KU-070-457

500 RECIPES
FOR BEDSITTER COOKERY

Marguerite Patten

HAMLYN

Cover photograph by Paul Williams

Published by Hamlyn Publishing,
a division of The Hamlyn Publishing Group Limited,
Bridge House, London Road, Twickenham,
Middlesex, England

© Copyright The Hamlyn Publishing Group Limited 1970

All rights reserved. No part of this publication may be
reproduced, stored in a retrieval system, or transmitted, in
any form or by any means, electronic, mechanical,
photocopying, recording or otherwise, without the
permission of Hamlyn Publishing.

First published 1970
Thirteenth impression 1986

ISBN 0 600 31234 8

Printed and bound in Great Britain by
R. J. Acford

Contents

Introduction

Some Useful Facts and Figures   4

Section 1
Cooking for one or more   5
Quantities of food   5
Shopping for food   5
Equipment that may help in your
    bedsitter   8
Keeping food hot   10
Keeping cookery smells away   10
Your store cupboard   10

Section 2
The pleasure of cooking   11
Hors d'oeuvre   12
Soups   18

Main dishes   21
Cooking with eggs   21
Cooking with cheese   26
Cooking with fish   29
Cooking with meat   49
Cooking with vegetables   63
Salads   71
Cooking with pasta   72
Cooking savoury rice dishes   76
Cold desserts and hot puddings   78
Cakes   87
Dishes to keep you fit   89
Dishes for special diets   92

Index   93

Introduction

This book is for those of you who live in a 'bed-sitter' and have to cook with limited equipment and utensils. The recipes are planned so they need neither elaborate preparation nor a range of 'pots and pans', but I hope you will agree that they provide appetising and interesting dishes. I believe that good food and enjoyable meals are important as a contribution towards good health, so I have chosen recipes which use the important protein foods and fresh vegetables wisely, and I have given suggestions on the discerning purchase of food. Many of you who live in a 'bedsitter' will be managing on a limited budget, so I have included many recipes using low-priced foods; there is particular mention of 'easy to digest' dishes for the older readers of this book.

Obviously you will wish to entertain your friends from time to time, so become well known for serving interesting main dishes (many of which are in this book) and colourful salads, for discovering economical and good wine or for an 'old-fashioned' tea or coffee party.

At the beginning of the book you will find brief descriptions of some of the equipment suitable for 'bedsitters'.

In one way cooking in a 'bedsitter' is a wonderful challenge – if you can provide interesting and nutritious meals under these circumstances, you have every right to regard yourself as a *very good cook*.

MARGUERITE PATTEN

Some Useful Facts and Figures

Notes on metrication

In case you wish to convert quantities into metric measures, the following tables give a comparison.

Solid measures

Ounces	Approx. grams to nearest whole figure	Recommended conversion to nearest unit of 25
1	28	25
2	57	50
3	85	75
4	113	100
5	142	150
6	170	175
7	198	200
8	227	225
9	255	250
10	283	275
11	312	300
12	340	350
13	368	375
14	396	400
15	425	425
16 (1 lb)	454	450
17	482	475
18	510	500
19	539	550
20 (1¼ lb)	567	575

Note: When converting quantities over 20 oz first add the appropriate figures in the centre column, then adjust to the nearest unit of 25. As a general guide, 1 kg (1000 g) equals 2·2 lb or about 2 lb 3 oz. This method of conversion gives good results in nearly all cases, although in certain pastry and cake recipes a more accurate conversion is necessary to produce a balanced recipe.

Liquid measures

Imperial	Approx. millilitres to nearest whole figure	Recommended millilitres
¼ pint	142	150
½ pint	283	300
¾ pint	425	450
1 pint	567	600
1½ pints	851	900
1¾ pints	992	1000 (1 litre)

Oven temperatures

The table below gives recommended equivalents.

	°C	°F	Gas Mark
Very cool	110	225	¼
	120	250	½
Cool	140	275	1
	150	300	2
Moderate	160	325	3
	180	350	4
Moderately hot	190	375	5
	200	400	6
Hot	220	425	7
	230	450	8
Very hot	240	475	9

Notes for American and Australian users

In America the 8-oz measuring cup is used. In Australia metric measures are now used in conjunction with the standard 250-ml measuring cup. The Imperial pint, used in Britain and Australia, is 20 fl oz, while the American pint is 16 fl. oz. It is important to remember that the Australian tablespoon differs from both the British and American tablespoons; the table below gives a comparison. The British standard tablespoon, which has been used throughout this book, holds 17·7 ml, the American 14·2 ml, and the Australian 20 ml. A teaspoon holds approximately 5 ml in all three countries.

Section 1

Cooking for one or more

Cooking for one

It can be dull cooking for just one person – if you allow it to be so. Never get into the habit of saying or thinking 'it is not worthwhile' – it is – for you *need* good food. Think of the consolations of cooking just for yourself; you can eat WHAT you like (no one else to consider) and you can eat WHEN you feel like it (although *very* irregular meals are often the cause of gastric or duodenal ulcers, so do not leave too long between meals). If you take an interest in food and new recipes you will soon have variety. Spend a little time 'shopping around', so you have an idea of where you can best buy smaller quantities of foods, for this is one of the difficulties of catering for one person. You are lucky today in that there is a great variety of convenience foods available in the shops, many of them being ideal for quick catering. Entertain as often as you can as eating in pleasant company is enjoyable.

Cooking for more than one

Maybe you are a couple who live in a 'bedsitter', in one way this is easier from the catering point of view, for shopping for two people instead of one enables you to buy reasonable quantities. On the other hand, it does mean that if your room is to remain pleasant and tidy you need to work very methodically, so take particular care to clear up as you prepare the food.

Quantities of food

Recipes for one person

Many recipes are given for one normal portion. Obviously if you use this dish when entertaining, you will need to multiply the ingredients for the number of people for whom you are catering, unless the recipe gives special suggestions for a larger quantity.

Recipes for two people

Some recipes are given for two people. This is because the dish is just as good if served a second time, so even when you are by yourself it is a practical recipe to try.

Shopping for food

If you are busy working you will have little time for shopping, so it is worthwhile making a list of the foods you need to save time and nothing is forgotten.

It is worthwhile looking around your neighbourhood to assess the food shops and see how they compare for quality (this of course includes the freshness of the food) and for price.

5

When comparing prices remember that good quality foods are the most economical for there is little waste and you will enjoy the food.

On the whole you are well advised to shop where a good trade is maintained, particularly when buying greengrocery and fruit, for this means the foods are bought daily by the owner. A rather quiet, less successful shop will often have food to sell which is not fresh.

To tell if foods are fresh

Meats and poultry

Bacon and cooked meats should never be hard and dry looking, it is advisable to buy bacon in polythene bags to keep it moist - check on the date to make sure you have a reasonable period of time before the bacon need be used.

Fresh meat should be moist looking, if dry and hard it has been exposed to the air for too long a period.

Beef should have some fat, as this shows a good quality and will give the meat a moist texture as well as being tender. The fat should always look firm and be a pale cream in colour, the lean meat should be bright red.

Lamb should have fairly transparent looking fat and the lean meat should be pale pink. Mutton is not mentioned in this book for it needs longer cooking than lamb, as it is more mature meat and is less suitable for your particular type of cooking.

Pork lean meat should be pale pink and very firm, with very firm white fat.

Veal has very little fat, but any fat should be white in colour and firm. The lean should also be firm and very pale pink.

Chicken should be white fleshed and firm looking. Today it is possible to buy joints of chicken (often frozen chicken) and most recipes deal with these, as a whole chicken, unless you are entertaining, could be too large.

Sausages and offal should be stored in a cool cabinet as they deteriorate more quickly than meat.

To store: if you have no refrigerator then it is better to buy fresh daily, as the warmth in a living room is possibly too great for meats, except when cooked – even then care must be taken to use fairly quickly. Bacon is salted and so it keeps longer.

Vegetables and fruits

Vegetables should be firm and fresh looking. Cabbages, etc., should be heavy for their size, with no yellow leaves on the outside; lettuce should be the same, also firm, green and crisp. The flower of cauliflower should be white and firm. Root vegetables should be as free from blemish as possible. It is worth buying pre-washed vegetables when living in a bedsitter, although these tend to deteriorate much more quickly than those that have not been washed. Fruits also should be firm and unbruised. When buying pears, tomatoes and other fruit that ripen quickly, ask for some that are under-ripe.

Punnets of soft fruit should not be moist on the bottom.

Dairy produce

Eggs today are rarely stale. If you are not satisfied with the eggs you buy, it is wise to change your supplier.

Cheese should not look dry on the outside.

Milk and cream should be bought from a store that keeps them in a refrigerated container. Pour into a vacuum flask to keep in hot weather.

Butter and margarine keep well, but salted butter keeps better than fresh.

Fish

This is a highly perishable food and it may be better to buy ready frozen fish; this will ensure no spoilage.

Fresh fish, however, should have a pleasant smell, beware of any fish that smells of ammonia. The scales, skin and eyes should look bright, not dull.

Convenience foods

This is the term given to dried, canned and frozen foods today. Fortunately dried foods keep well, so if you cannot use all the packet at once then the remainder will keep. It is possible to buy small sizes in most canned foods and reasonably small sizes in frozen foods. When a can of food has been opened or frozen food allowed to thaw out or be cooked, they are as perishable as fresh foods.

Milk and cream in convenient forms

It is possible to obtain milk in various forms that are all easily stored.

There is long lasting milk and cream – that

stores for some weeks in cartons and has the same taste as fresh milk or cream.

Canned milk and cream keep indefinitely before the can is opened – evaporated, non-sweetened milk is good in puddings or for drinks; the sweetened, condensed milk gives one or two interesting recipes in this book. Canned cream can be used in place of fresh.

Dried milk is an excellent standby, for you spoon just as much as you need from the can. The dried milk sold as babies food is full cream milk, but household dried milk has the food value of skimmed milk.

Yoghourt and dairy soured cream have been used in several recipes in this book, as they are highly nutritious and convenient foods.

Dried foods

Many of the dried foods one buys today are Accelerated Freeze Dried, which means they need no soaking before cooking. Follow the directions on the packets for use. Dried foods are obtainable in a selection of complete meals; in soups (ideal often to add flavour to a sauce or gravy), in vegetables, as well as packet mixes for desserts.

Cooking onions in a living room is not particularly pleasant, and dried onions, which keep in packets or tins, as well as other dried vegetables are wise investments for the 'bed-sitter' cook.

Dried cake mixes, pastry mixes, etc., are also good to use, for they help to give variety to your meals.

Canned foods

These give you an almost unending selection of every day and exotic foods from other countries. The following are useful:

Canned soups: to serve both as a soup or a gravy or sauce. The modern concentrated or 'condensed' soups are the best buy, for then you can dilute them with milk for a more nutritious soup or use them undiluted as a good consistency sauce. You can also buy sauces ready canned to serve with pasta if wished.

Canned fish: canned salmon, tuna, sardines, herrings, etc., have been used in many recipes in this book.

Canned meats: some of the nicest and most adaptable meats are corned beef, luncheon meat, ham, pork and ham, tongue, as well as canned stewing steak (in a variety of ways). You can also buy canned steak and kidney puddings and pies.

Canned vegetables: there are a wide selection including canned potatoes, carrots, mixed vegetables, asparagus, baked beans (a good source of protein), peas, etc. In addition, one can buy ready prepared potato and mixed vegetable salads. Remember canned vegetables only need heating through.

Canned fruits: most fruits are obtainable in cans. You can buy fruit purée (apple in particular), pie fillings (where the mixture is in a thickened liquid), other fruits in syrup, as well as fruit juices. Most canned foods can be left in the can, but the syrup of canned fruit tends to become cloudy, so turn out of the can when it is opened.

Naturally canned fruits and vegetables, because they have been subjected to heat, do not retain the same amount of vitamins as fresh fruits and vegetables.

Frozen foods

These have 'revolutionised' catering today, for the foods retain so much of the taste and texture of fresh foods. Some foods may be cooked from the frozen state, others need to thaw out (defrost) before using, follow directions regarding this and for storing the foods.

Frozen fish: look out for ready coated fish fillets, cutlets, fingers, etc., so you have no 'mess' with coating the fish before cooking. Most white fish can be cooked from the frozen state. Shellfish, however, must be allowed to defrost gradually before using, otherwise it is tough.

Frozen meats: meat cakes (hamburgers), chops, etc., can be cooked from the frozen state, but frozen chicken is better if allowed to thaw out before cooking.

Frozen vegetables: these should be cooked according to the timing on the packets. Do not over-cook the vegetables, since they are always very young and they are 'blanched', i.e. subjected to a certain amount of heat, before freezing, which shortens the cooking time.

Frozen fruits: allow these to defrost but use as soon as they are defrosted. In fact, frozen strawberries are at their best when they are faintly 'iced'.

Frozen pastry (see page 82): just roll out and use as fresh pastry.

Frozen cakes: allow to thaw out. When a frozen cake is filled with cream use up quickly as cream is highly perishable.

Ice cream: an ideal basis for many easy desserts.

Note:
To keep frozen foods as long as possible without a refrigerator, wrap the packet in several thicknesses of newspaper or put into a wide-necked vacuum flask.

Other ingredients for your store cupboard are given on pages 10 to 11.

Equipment that may help in your 'bedsitter'

Often you rent a room with the kitchen equipped or partially equipped. If, however, you are buying equipment, these are some of the things to consider:

The cooker itself

When you live, sleep and cook in one room, space (or often lack of space) is a problem.

Today, many 'bedsitters' have excellent 'tuck-away' kitchen corners.

A small complete cooker

It is possible to buy complete cookers, i.e. with boiling plates or rings, a grill and small oven. The following sketches, prices and measurements are fairly typical, so you can decide if you are sufficiently interested to visit your local Gas or Electricity Board or shops. The prices quoted are only approximate and must NOT be taken as *exact*. The measurements are also approximate.

Gas cooker

A small complete cooker can be purchased fairly easily today – gas cookers for 'bedsitters' look like Fig. 2.

Electric cooker

A small complete cooker can also be purchased easily, sometimes with a stand. It looks as the sketch and measures approximately $18\frac{1}{2}$ inches wide $\times$ $15\frac{1}{2}$ inches deep. It can be put on a table or purchased with a stand.

Note:

It is important to check that the small cooker you buy, needs only a 13 amp power socket and not a complete cooker circuit and cooker control panel.

The cooker illustrated is typical of small cookers that are quite safe plugged into the power circuit.

There are smaller models too, and those with a second hot plate. (Fig. 4).

The cooker on a cabinet

It may, however, be worthwhile either buying the cooker on a cabinet or having a cupboard (topped with heat resisting material), so that saucepans, crockery, etc., may be stored under this.

This has a great advantage that the cooker may be set at a convenient height, particularly for the elderly who may not be able to stoop down to an oven.

The grill boiler

If space does not permit having an oven then perhaps a combined grill and boiler may be the answer. This can be obtained either with gas or electricity and would look like Figs. 1 and 3.

The boiling ring or plate

Perhaps you feel that you can only afford a boiling ring or boiling plate. If possible buy a double one, for the difference in price is not so large and this gives you much greater scope for cooking.

More useful equipment

If you have limited cooking equipment you may find other utensils can be added gradually to save time and give more effective cooking facilities.

These may include an electric kettle, an electric percolator and an electric toaster or better still look at a toaster oven. This is especially useful if you only have gas or electric hotplates. It can be plugged into a 13 amp. power plug.

The cooking utensils you need

If you have just one boiling ring, it is a waste

of money buying a great selection of utensils you will not be able to use – here are basic and practical suggestions.

Saucepans: you can make use of two saucepans at one time, even with only one boiling ring (as you will see in the various recipes and menus). Choose two of at least 3 pint capacity so they are adaptable for various purposes.

When you buy them:

a choose as good a quality as you can afford; a heavier pan keeps food hotter when you move it off the ring; also food is less likely to stick.

b look at 'non-stick' pans which are easier to clean or the type of modern attractive 'oven-to-table' ware, which often have a detachable handle.

c make sure the pans have well fitting lids.

d look for pans with short handles that fit more easily into limited cupboard space. A milk saucepan is a good 'extra' but is far less versatile than an ordinary pan, since they are not made with lids.

Steamer: a one or two-tier steamer extends your cooking scope a great deal BUT does mean you will experience quite a lot of condensation in your room. If ventilation is *good* you may consider this worthwhile; if it is *bad* then you may not wish to buy one.

If you contemplate buying a steamer, make sure it fits securely on one of your saucepans.

Frying pan: today you can buy frying pans *with* lids so they 'do duty' as another saucepan. Here again follow suggestions (b) and (c) under saucepans.

Omelette pan: while a separate omelette pan may seem an extravagance, it is money wisely spent if you enjoy omelettes and pancakes. As in all probability you will be making omelettes for one person most of the time, buy a small sized omelette pan, 5 inches in diameter is ideal; too large an omelette pan means the small quantity of eggs are spread over too large an area and this gives a thin over-dry omelette.

Cake tin: this is not essential unless you wish to make a steamed cake as recipe page 87.

Sieve or colander: this is for straining vegetables, etc. Possibly a sieve is a better investment as it is more versatile.

If you have two boiling rings: add another

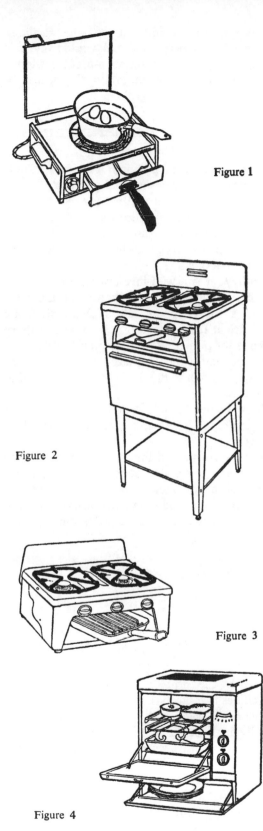

Figure 1

Figure 2

Figure 3

Figure 4

saucepan to extend your cooking facilities.
If you have boiling rings and a grill: invest in one or even two strong oven-proof casseroles where food, such as au gratin dishes, may be browned under the grill.

Utensils for preparing and serving food

When space is at a premium it is often possible to make many utensils 'dual-purpose'.

Basins: buy several pretty basins so they can be used for serving dishes as well as mixing foods – or you can use oven-proof decorated casseroles as serving dishes and as basins to prepare foods.

Cutlery: it is a wise investment to buy *one or two kitchen knives* so you do not use table knives for chopping, etc. Table knives are inefficient for this purpose. You need a sharp knife for preparing fruit and vegetables.

If you buy a medium sized knife, it will be strong enough to dice meat, etc., if you need to do this.

A flat-bladed knife (palette knife) is helpful for lifting foods from pans, etc., as well as a fish-slice.

Spoons are needed for stirring foods as they cook and a wooden spoon gives you better control over sauces and soups as you stir.

Grater: some kind of grater is always useful to grate cheese, carrots, onions, etc. (grated vegetables cook much more quickly than diced vegetables).

Lemon squeezer: for extracting fruit juices from the fruit.

Your china: If you are buying china for your bedsitting room, choose china that is not too fragile, especially in dinner plates, etc., for you may need to dish up foods quite early and keep them hot for a long period.

Some oven-proof ware can do double duty, as plates on which you can cook as well as serve the food.

Additional equipment to buy gradually

The equipment already mentioned is really the most essential, but other helpful items are:

Chopping board
Kitchen scissors
Perforated large spoon
Whisk
A small electric blender
Paper and foil in the kitchen
A kitchen paper roll is needed for:

a Draining fried food to absorb the excess grease.
b Wiping out greasy pans, etc., to make washing-up more pleasant.
c Wiping down all cooking surfaces, so you use the minimum of damp cloths.

You will also find the paper useful for rubbing polish on furniture.

Keeping foods hot

One of the problems with limited cooking facilities is to keep the food hot. This problem has been dealt with as far as possible in individual menus and recipes; but there are many inexpensive warming plates available and these can be a wise investment. Some use night lights for warmth instead of electricity.

Asbestos mats are quite inexpensive to buy and will protect your table from hot food.

Keeping cookery smells away

One of the problems when you cook in your living room is to keep the room smelling pleasant. Today there are a number of aerosol products to freshen the atmosphere when you cook. You may find it worthwhile investing in a small inexpensive extractor fan, if you intend to live in the premises for some considerable time.

Your store cupboard

You will need a few basic ingredients in your cupboard.

Ingredients that keep well:

Breadcrumbs: you can buy these dried in packets, they are used for coating fish, etc.

Canned foods: see comments on page 7.

Cocoa or drinking chocolate: these are used for drinks and also for flavouring cakes, puddings and sauces. In each recipe you are given the choice of cocoa or chocolate powder so you need buy one only, unless you have plenty of space.

Coffee: Ground coffee is necessary for making coffee in a percolator, and you will be given a wide choice of blends in a good store.

American roast is a light roast and ideal if you do not like coffee too dark and strong. Medium roast is good for most purposes. Continental roast is a darker roast and often contains some chicory which gives a strong taste.

Do buy small quantities of coffee if you have it freshly ground and store in a screw topped jar or tin. It is probably better to buy the vacuum packed tins of coffee. Instant coffee, however, enables you to make coffee very quickly and today this is of good flavour. It can also be used in cooking.

Cornflakes or other breakfast cereals: buy small packets and keep tightly covered so they remain crisp.

Cornflour: this is given as an alternative in many recipes for thickening stews and soups.

Dried or dehydrated vegetables, etc.: see page 7.

Flour: you will be offered the choice of plain or self-raising flour, the latter includes raising agents. I have used self-raising flour in all recipes in this book to save you stocking both.

Macaroni or spaghetti: if you intend to cook your own pasta, use these as they keep well.

Rice: keep a stock of long grain (often called Patna) rice or Italian rice – the latter is more difficult to obtain, but gives an excellent appearance as well as flavour in the various risottos on page 77.

Sugar: lump or loaf, preserving, granulated, castor, icing and various kinds of brown.

If you wish to buy one kind of sugar only, then select granulated or castor.

Tea: there are many teas from which you can choose.

You may find that although tea bags are more expensive to buy it is easier to dispose of them. Instant tea like instant coffee is also available.

Seasonings, flavourings: it is all too easy to be tempted to buy a large selection of flavourings, spices, herbs, etc., in shops today. Buy the essentials only and then add to these gradually.

Salt – this you will need in cooking and on the table. Buy salt in a container that looks attractive and excludes the air.

Pepper – there are several kinds of pepper. White pepper is for flavouring and table use, black pepper has a stronger flavour. If you have a pepper-mill, you should buy peppercorns. Cayenne pepper is very hot.

Paprika is often called a pepper, but in fact is not hot at all. It comes from the sweet red pepper and is excellent as a garnish.

Other good flavourings:

Worcestershire sauce – for tomato juice, etc.

Curry powder – if you like curries.

Powdered mixed herbs – to add to sauces, etc.

Separate herbs – the most useful are thyme, sage, parsley (instead of using fresh herbs).

Spices – powdered nutmeg and ginger.

Section 2

The pleasure of cooking

I hope you will enjoy preparing interesting meals for yourself and your friends.

In each chapter of this second section of the book, I have divided the foods into those you can buy ready-made and dress up and those you prepare from the beginning and which need some cooking.

This will enable you to make a quick selection according to the time available.

Hors d'oeuvre

Even when you are by yourself, a simple hors d'oeuvre can turn a somewhat dull meal into a more interesting one. When you entertain friends it will allow you to present a meal with a special look.

Hors d'oeuvre that need little attention

With fruit

For a very simple to prepare hors d'oeuvre serve canned or bottled fruit juices, canned or bottled tomato juice or canned or fresh grapefruit.

Fruit supreme

This is a pleasant American idea, not unlike a fruit salad, but keep fairly 'tart' in flavour to make it refreshing.

no cooking time

you will need for 2 servings :

1 small grapefruit   tiny can of pineapple
1 orange*   cubes (smallest size)

to decorate :
sprigs of mint when available

* Particularly good to do this when seedless Navel oranges are available.

1 Cut away the peel from the grapefruit and orange, so removing the inner white pith at the same time. Do this over a basin so no juice is wasted.
2 Cut the segments of fruit away from the skin. This takes a little practise, but if you have a good sharp knife it is not difficult. Discard any pips.
3 Open the can of pineapple and drain off the syrup. This must be discarded or used for another purpose – see fruit cocktails.
4 If the cubes or rings of pineapple are too large to eat with a teaspoon then slice neatly.
5 Mix the fruits together and put into 2 glasses or on 2 dishes. Top with mint. You may need to add sugar but the sweet pineapple and orange should be sufficient. If you have a refrigerator chill well before serving.

Note :
Other canned fruits you may use are apricots, lychees; most other fruits are too sweet to serve at the beginning of a meal.

Fruit cocktails

Mix together fresh or canned orange and/or grapefruit juice and canned pineapple juice or the syrup from canned pineapple. Obviously when you prepare this, you will make quite a generous quantity if you buy a can of each fruit juice, so wait until you have several guests before making fruit cocktails.

Grilled grapefruit

cooking time : few minutes
cooking appliance : grill

you will need for 2 servings :
1 large grapefruit   pinch mixed spice
½ oz. butter   or powdered nutmeg
2 teaspoons brown sugar
  or castor sugar

1 Halve the grapefruit, remove the centre pithy 'core'.
2 Separate the segments with a sharp knife and cut the fruit away from the skin at the edge, to make it easier to eat.
3 Spread the butter over the top.
4 Mix the sugar and spice or nutmeg and sprinkle over the top of the grapefruit.
5 Heat the grill for a few minutes then put the grapefruit under this.
6 Heat for a few minutes only (this does not destroy the Vitamin C in the fruit).
7 Serve at once.

To vary :
With honey and brown sugar : use honey or honey with brown sugar.
With sherry : sprinkle the fruit lightly with sherry before adding the butter.
With fruit juice : if the grapefruit is a little dry (this happens towards the end of the season sometimes), then sprinkle the fruit with bottled or fresh lime, lemon or orange juice, then spread with butter, etc.

With melon

There are seasons of the year when you can buy really small inexpensive melons, this is the time to buy them if you are cooking for yourself. To serve, cut the melon into halves, remove the centre seeds and serve with sugar and powdered ginger.

There are several ways to make the melon more interesting for guests

a **With orange:** cut the melon into thick slices. Cut the fruit pulp away from the skin with a sharp knife, then divide into segments so they are easy to eat. Put a slice of fresh orange on a cocktail stick and stick into the melon slices.

b **With wine or sherry:** halve the melon across, so when the seeds are removed you have two cup shapes. Sprinkle the centre with either a little white or red wine or sherry and sugar. Leave for about 1 hour to allow the flavour of the wine to impregnate the melon. Serve with extra sugar, but no ginger.

c **With grapefruit and orange:** halve the melon as above and fill the centre with segments of grapefruit and oranges – this is also delicious as a fruit salad.

d A very sophisticated and expensive hors d'oeuvre is to serve a portion of melon with smoked Parma ham – but if you know a good cooked meat shop, you can serve a slice of ordinary ham or even salami as an inexpensive alternative.

With tomatoes

There is always much discussion as to whether a tomato is a fruit or vegetable, but nevertheless it is excellent as a first course of a meal as well as part of a main course.

Tomato salad

Choose 1 large tomato per person (this will weigh about 3 oz.).

When tomatoes are at their best there is no need to skin them, but when the skin becomes tough you can remove this either:

a by putting the tomato into a saucepan or basin of very hot water for about 30 seconds. Remove it with a spoon and put it into cold water, so it does not become over-soft, then gently peeling or

b if you cook by gas, by inserting a fine skewer or fork into the tomato and holding it over the gas jet with the heat on, leaving for 2–3 seconds only until the skin breaks. The skin may then be pulled away gently.

Cut the tomato into thin slices and sprinkle with seasoning (salt and pepper), a pinch mixed herbs or freshly chopped parsley and a light sprinkling of oil and vinegar.

This sounds very simple but it is an excellent way to start a meal, and sliced tomatoes can, of course, be varied in many ways.

With anchovy fillets: top with anchovy fillets (one small can will be enough for 3–4 portions) – be sparing with salt as these are very salty.

With sardines: top with canned sardines (a small can will serve 3–4 portions).

With hard-boiled egg: top with chopped hard-boiled egg (allow 1 egg for 2 portions as an hors d'oeuvre – or 1 egg per person, if the next course is very light).

With cream cheese: top with cream cheese (allow 1 oz. per person) and chopped parsley or the chopped stalks of a few spring onions.

With ham: arrange strips of cooked ham and/or cooked tongue over the tomato (allow 1 oz. meat per person for an hors d'oeuvre or 2–3 oz. meat per person for a more filling dish).

Stuffed tomatoes are on pages 15–16.

With fish

Smoked fish is one of the most popular hors d'oeuvre today. Smoked salmon and smoked eel are relatively expensive but very delicious. Smoked mackerel and smoked trout are more reasonably priced.

Smoked eel: allow about 2 oz. per person. Serve with horseradish cream (obtainable in jars), brown bread and butter and slices or wedges of lemon, (a wedge of lemon is made by cutting the lemon in quarters).

An interesting garnish which enables you to serve a smaller portion, is to top the eel with cold scrambled egg – this is very popular in Scandinavia.

Smoked mackerel: allow 1 large smoked mackerel for about 3 portions. Serve as smoked eel.

Smoked trout: allow 1 fish per person. Serve as smoked eel. Eating the trout is made more simple if the fairly firm skin is removed. Do this just before serving.

Smoked salmon: allow 1–2 oz. per person, depending upon the choice of the main course. Serve with lemon, brown bread and butter and paprika or cayenne pepper.

Note:

Larger portions of the fish with salad are excellent as a main dish.

With meat

There is such a wide range of cooked meats today, that it is a good idea to serve these as hors d'oeuvre, if you are having a fish, egg or cheese main dish.

Various kind of salami: allow 1–2 oz. per person and serve with French bread or rolls and butter. Garnish with lettuce and wedges of tomato.

Pâté: one small can of pâté is enough for 2–3 people or allow 1–1½ oz. per person. Arrange the pâté on one or two lettuce leaves and garnish with wedges of tomato and/or lemon. Serve with hot toast if possible and butter, but where facilities for making toast are difficult serve with packet Melba toast, crisp-bread or slices of brown bread. Always serve the butter separately.

Mixed hors d'oeuvre

If you are entertaining sufficient people to justify the purchase of a fairly good selection of ingredients, then make up plates of mixed hors d'oeuvre.

a Some kind of vegetable – canned or fresh asparagus, sliced uncooked mushrooms.

b Tomatoes, sliced

c Some kind of fish – sardines, anchovies, smoked salmon

d Some kind of meat – salami, pâté

e Bottled olives and/or cocktail onions and/or gherkins

f Sliced hard-boiled eggs in mayonnaise, (see page 17)

Hors d'oeuvre needing more preparation or cooking

With vegetables

Asparagus

When asparagus is reasonably priced you may like to serve this as a special first course. It is often possible to buy asparagus by weight rather than in bundles, and allow about 4 oz. per portion.

Cut the bottom from the stalks of asparagus and scrape the white stalks gently with a knife, then wash in cold water. Be careful not to break the delicate tips.

The ideal pan for cooking asparagus is a tall one, to allow the asparagus to stand upright. Tie the asparagus in bundles with fine string, so the stalks do not 'flop' in the water and the tips become damaged, or cook as frozen asparagus below. Add a little salt and cook steadily until just tender, this takes about 20 minutes for fairly thin stalks up to about 25–30 minutes for very thick ones. Lift out carefully and strain. Put on to a hot serving plate or dish and serve hot with melted butter or cold with French or vinaigrette dressing, see page 16.

Frozen asparagus: choose a wide pan if possible or even a deep frying pan. Put in the frozen asparagus with salt to taste and cook as directed on the packet.

Canned asparagus: open the can at both ends, this enables you to pull the stalks of the asparagus out from the base of the can so there is less chance of the heads being damaged. Heat in the liquid from the can for a few minutes, then drain and serve with melted butter or just open the can, drain and serve cold with French dressing or as suggested below.

To drain asparagus: do not tip into a sieve or colander – lift out with a fish slice and hold over the pan so the asparagus drains well.

New ways to serve asparagus

With cheese: put the hot asparagus into a shallow oven-proof dish, top with a thick layer of grated Cheddar or Parmesan cheese, a few crisp breadcrumbs and a little butter. Heat under the hot grill.

With cream cheese: blend a little mayonnaise, salad cream or dairy soured cream into the cream cheese. Put the cold asparagus on to a bed of crisp lettuce and top with the cheese mixture. Allow 1 oz. cheese per portion and enough mayonnaise, etc., to make the consistency of a thick cream.

à la Polonaise : cover the hot asparagus with melted butter and then with chopped hard-boiled egg, or top the cold asparagus with mayonnaise and chopped hard-boiled egg. Allow 1 egg for 2 portions.

Asparagus and ham rolls : allow 2–3 heads of asparagus per person and 1–1½ oz. cooked ham per portion. Moisten the cold asparagus with a little oil and vinegar, lay on strips of cooked ham and roll the ham round these. Serve on a bed of lettuce.

Artichoke

A globe artichoke, i.e. the green type of artichoke, makes an excellent and not too expensive hors d'oeuvre.

The vegetable should be green in colour. If the leaves are turning brown and dry then it is stale. Wash in plenty of cold water before cooking. Cut away the stalk to the level of the base of the leaves, remove a few outer leaves if they look slightly big (and therefore a little tough). Put into enough boiling salted water to cover and cook steadily for approximately 30 minutes. Test by inserting a knife at the base, this should be tender.

To serve hot : the tips of the leaves may be trimmed before cooking if wished. When the artichoke is cooked, lift it out of the pan with a perforated or large spoon, and allow it to drain for a moment. Heat 1–1½ oz. butter. To eat the artichoke, pull off the leaves and eat the fleshy base of each leaf, dipping it into the hot butter. In the centre of the artichoke is the 'choke' which is not eaten, but the fleshy base is eaten with a knife and fork.

To serve cold : cook as above, drain and cool. Cut the tops from the leaves leaving them about ½–¾ inch in depth. Remove the centre 'choke'. Make a vinaigrette dressing (see under avocado pear, page 16) and pour this into the middle cavity. To eat the artichoke, pull off each leaf and dip this into the vinaigrette dressing, then eat the base with a knife and fork.

Stuffed tomatoes – cooked

cooking time : 10 minutes
cooking appliance : oven

you will need for 2 servings :

2 large tomatoes	seasoning

for the filling :

1 egg	2 small gherkins
1 oz. grated Parmesan cheese (approximately)	½ oz. butter (small knob)

1 Cut a slice from each tomato – if you take this from the end opposite to the stalk you will find the tomatoes stand upright.
2 Scoop out the centre pulp with a teaspoon. Put this on to a plate and cut the core with a sharp knife so it is a fairly fine mixture.
3 Tip this into a basin. Season the tomato case and the pulp in the basin.
4 Add the egg, cheese, chopped gherkins and blend well. Put into the tomato cases.
5 Butter an oven-proof serving dish or use an oven-proof plate.
6 Stand the tomatoes in this and replace the slice cut from each tomato, add the tiny amount of butter left to the top of each tomato.
7 Bake in the centre of a hot oven (425–450°F., Gas Mark 6–7) until just tender. Serve hot or cold.

To vary :

a **Using the grill instead of the oven :** stand the tomatoes in the grill pan and cook steadily until soft – place the grill pan as far as possible away from the direct heat of the grill, so the tomato filling becomes cooked as well as the tomatoes.
b **With prawns :** omit the cheese and add prawns – buy 2 oz. shelled prawns. Mix just over 1 oz. chopped prawns with the egg and tomato pulp, save the rest for garnish on top of the tomatoes.
c **With ham :** omit the cheese and use finely chopped ham – allow 1–1½ oz. lean meat.
d **Soufflé tomatoes :** use the mixture in the basic recipe, but separate the egg white from the yolk. Blend the yolk with the cheese, etc., whisk the egg white until very stiff, then fold into the mixture. Bake as before or cook under the grill.

Note :

Stuffed tomatoes also make a good main dish with a salad or vegetables, as well as an interesting looking hors d'oeuvre. Choose really firm tomatoes whether they are being heated or served raw. This enables you to cut the slice from the top without the tomato losing its shape.

Stuffed tomatoes – uncooked

Buy 2 large firm tomatoes and cut a slice from each tomato – taking this from the end opposite to the stalk so the tomatoes stand upright. Scoop out the centre pulp, chop this finely and put into a basin. Blend the pulp with:

a 1 chopped, hard-boiled egg, 1 oz. grated cheese, seasoning.

b 1 chopped, hard-boiled egg, a little mayonnaise and 1 or 2 chopped gherkins.

c 1–1½ oz. diced Cheddar or Gruyère cheese, good shake of salt, pepper, ½–1 teaspoon made mustard, little chopped cucumber or diced gherkins to flavour.

d flaked canned fish (salmon, tuna, sardines, anchovies are all good) or chopped cooked meat (beef, ham, tongue, etc.) in place of the diced cheese in c.

Pile the pulp back into the lightly seasoned tomato cases and stand the tomatoes on a bed of lettuce or watercress. Allow 1 tomato per person for an hors d'oeuvre or 2 tomatoes for a main dish.

With avocado pears

Avocado pears have become a very popular hors d'oeuvre during the past years. They are a wise buy for people with limited cooking facilities for they are a good source of protein (this is unusual in a fruit) and can be served uncooked as part of a salad as well as an hors d'oeuvre.

To buy a good avocado look critically at the outside green skin, it should be unblemished. If you wish to serve the avocado the day you buy it, it should feel soft to the touch at the stalk end, but if very soft it is likely to be too ripe. Should you buy an avocado that is under-ripe keep it in a warm place to hasten ripening – an airing cupboard is ideal, or near the cooker. If the pear is ripe it should be eaten the same day, unless you have a refrigerator in which it can be stored. Put it as far away from the freezing compartment as possible. Bring the avocado pear out of the refrigerator at least an hour before serving, since it should not be too cold. A medium-sized avocado is enough for an hors d'oeuvre for two people, unless being followed by a very light main dish when 1 small pear could serve one person.

The simplest way of serving the pear is given below – with an oil and lemon or vinegar dressing – but there are many other ways to serve this and further suggestions follow.

Avocado pear with vinaigrette dressing

no cooking

you will need for 2 servings :

1 medium ripe avocado
  pear*

for the dressing :

juice ½ – 1 lemon or
  approximately ½
  tablespoon vinegar
1 tablespoon olive
  or corn oil

pinch dry mustard
  (optional)
shake pepper
shake salt
good pinch sugar

to garnish :

lettuce leaves
  (not essential)

* An avocado is really a fruit but quite unlike an ordinary pear.
Vinaigrette dressing is sometimes known as French dressing.

1 Halve the avocado pear lengthways and remove the stone from the one part without damaging the flesh. If necessary, ease the stone from the flesh with the tip of a sharp knife. Only do this a short time before serving, since the avocado pear flesh discolours with exposure to the air.

2 Squeeze the juice from the lemon and sprinkle a few drops over the avocado pear to keep it moist while you prepare the dressing.

3 Blend the oil with the seasonings and sugar, then add enough lemon juice (or vinegar if preferred) to give a sharp flavoured dressing.

4 Put each half of the pear on to a small plate, garnish with a lettuce leaf and pour the dressing into the centre cavity. Serve with a teaspoon.

With prawns : buy 2 oz. shelled frozen prawns and allow these to defrost at room temperature. Blend the prawns with mayonnaise or mayonnaise to which a little tomato ketchup or tomato purée (purchase this in a tube) has been added. Halve the avocado pears and fill with the prawn mixture. Other shellfish, e.g., canned or frozen crab, lobster, could be used instead.

Avocado canapés

Buy a ripe pear and halve, remove the stone, then scoop out the centre pulp carefully taking care not to include any skin. Put the pulp into a basin and mash this. Add about 2 teaspoons lemon juice or vinegar, salt, pepper, shake cayenne pepper if available and about 1 teaspoon oil. Other flavourings you can use are a few drops Worcestershire sauce or a very little French mustard.

To serve as an hors d'oeuvre: slice 1 large tomato and pile the mixture on top of this or slice part of a cucumber and arrange likewise. One good sized pear will make an hors d'oeuvre for 2–3 portions prepared in this way. For a party, the soft pulp should be put on to cocktail biscuits.

Curried avocado pears and prawns

Prepare the avocado pear as for the canapés, but be very careful you do not damage the skin of the two halves as you remove the pulp. Mash the pulp in a basin adding a little curry powder to taste ($\frac{1}{2}$–1 teaspoon is enough for most people), 1 teaspoon oil, salt and pepper. Pile this back into the shells. Top each shell with 1 oz. prawns (use either defrosted, frozen, shelled prawns or canned prawns).

To serve cold: blend a good pinch curry powder with 2 tablespoons mayonnaise and coat the prawns with this.

To serve hot: top the prawns with a sprinkling of crisp breadcrumbs and either heat for a few minutes in the oven or under the grill.

If you do not like prawns, then other fish could be used.

See also avocado and cream cheese salad – page 72, which could also be served as an hors d'oeuvre if wished.

With salads

In addition to the tomato salad, page 13 and the simple salads given below, many of the recipes in the salad section pages 71 to 72 are excellent for hors d'oeuvre. The quantity given for one person would be sufficient for two people, though, as an hors d'oeuvre.

Egg mayonnaise

Allow 1 egg per person. Halve lengthways and coat with mayonnaise. Top with chopped parsley and paprika pepper to give a touch of colour, and arrange either on lettuce or garnished with a ring of sliced tomato.

Egg and sardine mayonnaise

Arrange 2 sardines on sliced tomato or lettuce. Top with sliced egg (allow $\frac{1}{2}$–1 egg per person) and a little mayonnaise.

Egg and anchovy salad

The smallest can of anchovy fillets is enough for 3–4 portions, so do not make this unless you are having friends to a meal, or have a refrigerator to keep the remainder of the canned fish. Allow 1 egg per person, halve and arrange on sliced cucumber, tomato or lettuce. Top with mayonnaise and arrange several anchovy fillets over the halved eggs.

Egg and prawn mayonnaise

Allow 1 egg and 1 oz. prawns (canned or frozen) per person. Hard-boil the eggs, shell and halve lengthways. Remove the yolks from the whites. Blend the prawns with the chopped yolks, mayonnaise to bind and pile back into the white cases. Serve on lettuce or sliced tomato or cucumber.

With eggs

In addition to the egg salads given on page 71, egg dishes are often an excellent hors d'oeuvre. They are light to eat and, therefore, do not spoil one's appetite for the main dish. They are not too strong in flavour and do not detract from the taste of the main dish. Follow the directions for egg dishes on pages 21 to 25 but allow only 1 egg per person.

With cheese

With the exception of a few dishes, i.e. pasta with cheese, rice with cheese or eggs and fish in a cheese sauce, it is not usual to serve cheese dishes as the first course for they are fairly substantial and also have a very definite flavour, which would spoil the taste of the main dish to follow.

With fish

Smoked fish, as page 13, are excellent as an hors d'oeuvre, so are all scampi and prawn and other fish dishes. Follow the suggestions on pages 38 to 39, but allow half portions as a first course.

With meat and poultry

These are less suitable to start a meal with the exception of chicken liver risotto, page 78, pâté and chopped liver, given below.

Chopped liver

Allow 2 oz. calf's or chicken's liver per person (this is a fairly generous amount, so could be reduced if wished). Fry the liver gently until just tender. Chop finely, serve on a bed of lettuce topped with chopped hard-boiled egg. Serve with French bread and butter or hot toast and butter.

Soups

There is nothing easier to prepare than home-made soup if one makes use of modern stock cubes, and canned or dehydrated soups as the base. Many of the prepared soups are excellent without adding other flavours, but one tends to tire of these, so in this chapter there are ideas to turn these into something more individual. You can sometimes buy very small cans of soup, suitable for one person, but the average size gives two portions. It is suggested, therefore, that you use half the can one day as a basic soup, adding no extra flavour, then use the second half of the can as the basis for a more imaginative soup, or to give you the sauce for a stew, etc. Naturally you cannot do this in very hot weather, for when once the can is opened the food is perishable.

Dehydrated soups are sold in packets, each packet making enough soup for 4–5 portions, so just use a quarter of the packet with the appropriate amount of water.

Stock cubes added to water gives you an excellent base for soups, stews, etc.

Here are some very quick and easy soups to make – the amount of soup is generous for one person, so could give 2 small portions if wished. As all soups given in this chapter just need heating or simmering, obviously the appliance used throughout is a boiling ring.

Fish soup

This is a very easy way of serving fish as a light meal.

cooking time: 10 minutes
cooking appliance: boiling ring

you will need for 1 serving:

1 small fillet plaice or a small portion other white fish – no more than 3 oz.	¼ pint water pinch mixed herbs seasoning, optional
½ chicken stock cube	
¼ pint milk	

to garnish:

chopped parsley or strips of tomato

1 Cut the fish into small pieces, removing the skin and any bones if not using fillet.
2 Put the stock cube into the pan with the milk and water, bring to the boil. Add the pieces of fish and simmer until just tender, adding the herbs and any seasoning required.
3 Top with the parsley or strips of tomato just before serving.

To make a thicker soup, add a small peeled grated potato and/or a little grated carrot with the fish. A very small amount of grated onion could also be used.

Bacon and tomato chowder *

cooking time: 10 minutes
cooking appliance: boiling ring

you will need for 1 serving:

1 rasher bacon (back or streaky)	1 chicken stock cube
½ oz. butter	½ pint water

1 small onion or use
dehydrated onion

2 medium tomatoes

to thicken:

1 small slice bread
without crusts
seasoning

* The word 'chowder' is American for a thick soup which produces a light meal by itself.

1 Remove rind from the bacon and put it into the saucepan. Add the chopped bacon and fry for a few minutes with the peeled, chopped or grated onion. If using dehydrated onion follow the directions.

2 Add the butter and the skinned, chopped tomatoes when the onion is nearly soft, remove the bacon rind.

3 Put in the stock cube and the water and bring to the boil and simmer for a few minutes, then add the crumbled bread and stir into the soup until it is blended with the liquid, so giving a thicker texture. Season if wished, although the stock cube gives a good amount of salt, etc.

To vary:

a Use canned consommé instead of stock cube and water.

b **Prawn and tomato chowder:** omit the bacon, fry the onion and tomatoes in 1 oz. butter. Stir in the stock cube and water, the crumbs and finally 1–2 oz. shelled prawns. These should be allowed to defrost if using frozen prawns, since the fish becomes very tough if it is heated from the frozen state.

Bacon and potato chowder

cooking time: 10 minutes
cooking appliance: boiling ring

you will need for 1 serving:

1 rasher bacon
(back or streaky)

1 onion or use
dehydrated onion

½ oz. butter

½ chicken stock cube

½ pint water or milk
and water

1 tablespoon dehydrated
potato powder
seasoning, optional

to garnish:

chopped parsley or
watercress

1 Remove rind from the bacon and put into the saucepan. Add the chopped bacon and fry for a few minutes with the peeled, chopped or grated onion. If using dehydrated onion follow the directions.

2 Add the butter, stock cube and liquid and remove the bacon rind.

3 Heat the liquid, remove from the heat, add the potato powder, blend smoothly, season if wished.

4 Top with parsley or watercress.

Mushroom soup

cooking time: 10 minutes
cooking appliance: boiling ring

you will need for 2 servings:

4 oz. mushrooms

1 oz. butter or
margarine

1 chicken stock cube

¾ pint water

seasoning, optional

1 Wash and slice the mushrooms fairly finely.

2 Toss in the butter or margarine for 2–3 minutes, then add the stock cube with the water and any seasoning required.

3 Bring to the boil, lower the heat and simmer for about 6 minutes until tender.

To vary:

Beef and mushroom soup: either use a beef stock cube or canned beef consommé instead.

Cream of mushroom soup: as above, but blend 2 teaspoons cornflour with 4 tablespoons cream from the top of the milk and stir this into the cooked soup and continue stirring over a low heat until thickened.

Carrot soup

Follow the directions for the quick vegetable soup below, but use all carrots.

Vegetable soup

cooking time: 15 minutes
cooking appliance: boiling ring

you will need for 2 servings:

1 oz. butter or
margarine

2 medium or 1 large
carrot

1 medium potato

1 medium onion

1 large tomato

¾ pint water

seasoning

1 Heat the butter or margarine in a saucepan and toss the peeled, grated carrot, potato and onion in this for about 5 minutes.

2 Add the skinned, chopped tomato and water. Bring to the boil, lower the heat and simmer gently for about 10 minutes, seasoning to taste.

To vary:

With cheese: top with grated cheese just before serving.

Cream of vegetable soup: use only ½ pint water. Blend 2 teaspoons cornflour with ¼ pint milk, thin cream or cream from the top of the milk. Add to the cooked soup, stirring well, and simmer for several minutes. Stir well and do not boil, otherwise the tomato could curdle the milk or cream.

Vegetable purée soup: as above, but rub through a sieve then reheat with a little cream or milk if wished.

Instead of fresh vegetables you can use frozen mixed vegetables and cook these.

Tomato vegetable soup: omit the fresh tomato and use canned or bottled tomato juice instead of water. Care must be taken though if thickening with milk or cream, that the mixture does not boil, otherwise the soup could curdle.

Quick ideas with canned or dehydrated soup

As well as canned soup you can use dehydrated soups, where you blend the soup powder with the required amount of water and simmer according to the directions on the packet. The amounts given below are for one person, so you would use either ½ medium sized can of soup or ¼ packet of soup powder.

Asparagus and ham chowder

Heat ½ can asparagus soup, add 1 oz. chopped cooked ham and a little chopped green pepper or red pepper (optional).

Asparagus and tuna chowder

This is worth making for two to three people as a special soup.

Heat a whole can of asparagus soup, then add flaked tuna fish (buy the smallest size can available), and garnish with chopped parsley or sprigs of watercress. Serve each cup with a generous wedge of lemon.

Canned salmon could be used instead.

Borsch

Put ½ can consommé into a saucepan, add 2–3 tablespoons finely chopped or grated, cooked beetroot and a few drops of lemon juice or vinegar. Serve hot, topped with plain yoghurt or dairy soured cream, or serve cold topped with yoghurt or cream cheese. Instead of a can of consommé, use 1 beef stock cube and ½ pint water.

Consommé plus

Canned consommé or beef or chicken stock cubes can be made into a more interesting soup if:

a flavoured with sherry or a little white wine (use a dry wine).

b a small amount of canned or cooked vegetables are added.

c you dilute the consommé or stock cube with rather more water than usual, and simmer ½–1 oz. rice in this. Flavour with sherry.

d heat the consommé in a fairly large saucepan or frying pan, then poach an egg in this for each person. Lift the egg into the soup bowl, add a little sherry and chopped parsley to the consommé and spoon over the egg.

Serve with lots of French bread.

Corn tomato soup

Add a tiny can of corn to ½ can tomato soup and heat for a few minutes. Top with grated cheese just before serving.

Corn and chicken soup

Use cream of chicken instead of tomato soup, add the corn and heat in this. Top with chopped parsley or sprigs of watercress instead of cheese.

Curried soup

A mulligatawny soup has a curry flavour. This can be made more interesting, if you fry a chopped onion in the pan in a little butter, then work in ½–1 teaspoon curry powder. Add ½ can mulligatawny soup and heat, diluting this with a little water or milk if it seems too thick.

Instead of using mulligatawny soup, you may use canned lentil soup or green pea soup as a base for this.

Main dishes

It is very important to choose your main dish with care, it should be based on protein foods. There are a wide variety of foods in which protein is to be found, so this gives you plentiful scope. I have put eggs and cheese first since they are ideal when you are in a hurry. They enable you to prepare light delicious meals with the minimum of time and effort.

Cooking with eggs

An egg provides excellent food value in an easily prepared and digested way – so make sure you have a reasonable supply of eggs available for quick meals or snacks.

Baked eggs

This is an easy way to cook eggs if you have an oven. Use small oven-proof dishes.

cooking time: 10-15 minutes
cooking appliance: oven

you will need for 1 serving:

½ oz. butter	seasoning
2 eggs	1 tablespoon thin cream or milk

1 Use half the butter to grease the dish.
2 Break the eggs carefully on the butter, add the seasoning, cream and remainder of the butter.
3 Bake for 10 minutes in a very moderate to moderate oven (350–375°F., Gas Mark 3–4) if you like the eggs lightly set or longer for a firmer egg. Serve with a teaspoon.
Note:
For an hors d'oeuvre, use 1 egg only but the same amount of cream to give a good covering.
To vary:
Eggs and cheese: put about 1 oz. grated cheese under and above the eggs before cooking.
Eggs with vegetables: spread a layer of thickly sliced, skinned tomato under the eggs or use sliced, cooked mushrooms, canned asparagus. Bake as above.

Swiss eggs

cooking time: 8-10 minutes
cooking appliance: oven

you will need for 1 serving:

2 eggs	2 oz. cheese
seasoning	1 oz. butter

to garnish:
1 sliced tomato

1 Beat the eggs with the seasoning, add finely grated cheese.
2 Spread half the butter in the dish, add the egg and cheese mixture and top with rest of butter in tiny pieces. Set as baked eggs.
3 Garnish with sliced tomato.

Boiled eggs

If the eggs are very fresh, allow 4 minutes for a lightly boiled egg. If you have had them in the house for some days, 3½ minutes are enough. Put several inches of cold water into small saucepan and bring to boil, then gently lower in the eggs and allow the water to boil gently. Lift out immediately at end of the cooking time. Some people prefer eggs boiled by putting them into boiling water, leaving them in covered pan OFF the heat for 7–8 minutes. This gives very light egg really called a coddled egg, not boiled. For a hard-boiled egg allow 10 minutes in boiling water. The moment the hard-boiled egg comes out of the boiling water put it into cold water. This prevents the dark line forming round the yolk due to over-cooking. Tap the egg firmly to crack the shell and it will come away easily.

To use soft-boiled eggs

Soft-boiled eggs should be put into cold water as suggested under hard-boiled eggs.
a **For a quick meal:**
Slices of cold ham are delicious topped with shelled soft-boiled eggs.
b **As a quick savoury:**
Shell eggs, put in dish, coat with little tomato

ketchup, top with plenty of grated cheese, put under hot grill for 1 minute.

c As a sandwich filling:

Shell the eggs and chop in a basin, add little salt, pepper and knob of butter. Spread over bread which needs light buttering only. Top with sprigs of watercress, mustard and cress or lettuce. This gives a very moist sandwich filling.

To use hard-boiled eggs

As easy savouries:

1 Shell the eggs, arrange in shallow dish, top with quick cheese sauce – see page 74 – and grated cheese and brown under grill.

2 Shell, put on bed of lettuce, top with canned anchovy fillets and a little mayonnaise.

3 Shell hard-boiled eggs while still slightly warm, cut through centre, remove yolks gently with a teaspoon and put into a basin. Mash with a fork and add:

a a few boned sardines, pinch pepper and salt

b chopped cooked ham and seasoning

c little grated cheese and chutney

d little anchovy essence – DO NOT salt

e little butter, good pinch curry powder, salt, pepper

Pile flavoured yolks back into white cases. Serve on bed of lettuce.

In sandwiches:

Shell and cut in neat slices or chop, arrange on bread and butter, season lightly; top with bread and butter or add sliced tomato, cucumber, mashed sardines, little mustard and cress, lean ham.

Eggs Mornay

While poached eggs are often used for this dish, I think it has more flavour with lightly boiled eggs. It is easy to do if you only have one ring. If you have one pan only, make the cheese sauce as page 74 (i.e. the white sauce without the cheese). Put it on one side while you boil the eggs.

Plunge the eggs into cold water and crack the shells. Remove the shells the moment they are sufficiently cool to handle. Put the eggs into a shallow dish. Warm the sauce, add the grated cheese and heat thoroughly. Pour over the eggs and serve at once.

If you have a grill: put for 2 or 3 minutes under a hot grill.

If you have an oven: put into a moderately hot oven for about 5–6 minutes.

Eggs Florentine

This dish is made with poached or soft-boiled eggs, spinach and cheese.

If you have one boiling ring only:

Make the cheese sauce as page 74 (i.e. the white sauce without the cheese). Put on one side. Boil the eggs, see Eggs Mornay.

Next cook the spinach in a second saucepan, drain carefully and return to the saucepan. Add the cheese to the sauce and heat thoroughly.

Put the hot spinach in the dish, add the shelled eggs, top with hot cheese sauce and serve.

If you have a grill: put for 2 or 3 minutes under the grill.

If you have an oven: put into a moderately hot oven for about 5–6 minutes.

Eggs with tomato cheese sauce

cooking time: 8-12 minutes
cooking appliance boiling ring

you will need for 2 servings:

4 eggs	4 oz. Cheddar cheese
medium can tomato soup concentrated consistency	

1 Either hard-boil or soft-boil the eggs, crack the shells and remove.

2 Put the eggs into a dish while heating the soup.

3 When the soup is hot, add the grated cheese, stir for 2–3 minutes and pour over the eggs. Serve at once.

Barbecued eggs

Make the barbecued sauce as page 61.

Hard-boil and shell the eggs and top with the hot sauce.

Serve with a salad or green vegetable.

Curried eggs

Make the curry sauce as page 58, omit meat.

Hard-boil and shell the eggs and put into the sauce and simmer for about 5 minutes. Serve with boiled rice or with a green salad.

Devilled eggs

Make the devilled sauce as page 39.
Hard-boil and shell the eggs and put into the devilled sauce.
This is equally good as a hot or cold dish. If serving cold the flavour is much better if the hot eggs stand in the hot sauce and they cool together.

Tuna eggs

cooking time: 12 minutes
cooking appliance: boiling ring

you will need for 2 servings:
4 eggs

for the sauce:

1 oz. butter or margarine	½ pint milk smallest size can
1 oz. flour or ½ oz. cornflour	tuna fish seasoning

1 Hard-boil, crack and shell the eggs.
2 Make the white sauce as page 74 with the butter, flour or cornflour and milk.
3 Add the tuna fish and beat well to break up the pieces of fish, season.
4 Put the hard-boiled eggs into the serving dish and top with the very hot sauce.

Fried eggs

If frying eggs with bacon, cook the bacon and either move to one side of the pan or put on a hot plate in the oven, or serve on a hot dish and keep hot on a plate warmer.
Break 1 egg into a cup or saucer, check to see there is a light coating of hot fat in the pan. If the bacon is very lean you may need to add extra fat before cooking the eggs. Lower the first egg into the pan and tilt it as you do so, to make sure the egg white sets neatly. The moment the egg white begins to set, add the second egg and continue in the same way. If you like the yolk covered with white, spoon a little fat over it while cooking. Set for about 3 minutes then lift out of the pan.
To serve fried eggs: serve the eggs with bacon, sausages, on baked beans, spaghetti.
Browned eggs
A simple and interesting variation on fried eggs is to cook the eggs in butter. Lift them on to a hot plate and heat any butter left in the pan until it becomes golden brown. Pour over eggs.

Poached eggs

Break the egg into a cup. Put a small knob of butter or margarine into the cup of an egg poacher or an old cup, which is standing in a pan of boiling water. Slide in the egg, put on a lid and boil water gently for 3½–4 minutes *or* slide the egg into boiling salted water in a saucepan or frying pan, adding ½–1 teaspoon of vinegar.* Cook for 3 minutes until white is set.

* This prevents egg white spreading, but some people dislike the taste.

Serve poached eggs
a on hot buttered toast;
b on toast – top with thin slices of cheese or grated cheese, brown under hot grill;
c on heated canned spaghetti, baked beans or cooked spinach.

Savoury poached eggs

cooking time: 15 minutes
cooking appliance: boiling ring

you will need for 1 serving:

1 oz. butter	seasoning
1 onion	¼ pint water
2 tomatoes	2 eggs

to garnish:
2 slices bread

1 Heat the butter in a frying pan or saucepan and cook the peeled and thinly sliced onion and skinned tomatoes until soft.
2 Season well, add the liquid and stir to give a thick purée.
3 Break the eggs carefully into this and set for about 3 minutes.
4 Put the bread or toasted bread on to a hot plate and top with the eggs and vegetables.
To vary:
With wine: if about 2 tablespoons wine are added to the water, this is very delicious for a special hors d'oeuvre for two people.
Poached egg on haddock
If you cook smoked haddock or cod it can be turned into a more interesting dish if topped with a poached egg.

Egg poachers: you can buy egg poachers with metal 'cups' for one, two or four people. They cost from about 3/6d. Wash as an ordinary pan. Store carefully with 'cups' in position.

Scrambled eggs

They should be creamy and moist. Never over-cook or cook too quickly.

Allow 1–2 eggs, 1 dessertspoon milk, seasoning, ½–1 oz. butter or margarine per person. Beat eggs with milk and seasoning. Heat the butter or margarine in saucepan, pour in mixture. Cook gently, stirring well until just set. Put on hot buttered toast.

Note :

It is advisable to prepare the toast before cooking the eggs, so they are not over-cooked.

Flavourings for scrambled egg

Add just before mixture is set:

a **cheese:** good tablespoon grated cheese
b **meat:** little chopped cooked ham or chicken
c **fish:** little flaked cooked fish or few prawns.

To clean pans after cooking eggs

Wash out well – after scrambling eggs, soak pan for a while in cold NOT hot water. Pour away and wash in usual manner. If using a 'non-stick' pan, the egg mixture left is easily removed.

To make omelettes

For a substantial serving allow 2 eggs per person and, if making omelettes for a number of people, do not try and cook too many eggs at a time. It is better to use 4–6 eggs at the maximum, i.e. an omelette for two or three people, in a 7–8 inch pan. If you try to cook a larger number, the process is too slow and the eggs tend to toughen.

For a plain or French type of omelette, whisk the eggs lightly with seasoning, adding a little water if wished. Allow about 1 dessertspoon water to each egg. Heat a good knob of butter or spoonful of oil in the omelette pan, put in the whisked eggs and allow to set lightly on the bottom. Then work the mixture by loosening the omelette from the sides of the pan, at the same time tilting it so that the liquid mixture flows underneath. Continue until all liquid has

set. Fold or roll away from the handle and tip on to a hot dish. Serve immediately.

For a soufflé omelette, the whites and yolks are separated and the stiffly beaten whites folded into the beaten yolks, then seasoned. This tends to be a drier, but of course a thicker and lighter omelette. It can be set without turning if, given a minute or so cooking in the usual way, it is then put under a moderately hot grill; or even finished cooking in the oven if the handle of the pan permits. While a soufflé omelette may be filled with savoury ingredients as suggested, they are more often served as a sweet.

Plain omelette

cooking time : few minutes
cooking appliance : boiling ring

you will need for 1 serving :

2 eggs	seasoning
1 tablespoon water	¾ oz. butter

1 Whisk eggs, water and seasoning lightly.
2 Heat the butter in a small omelette or frying pan.
3 Pour in the beaten eggs. Allow to set lightly on the bottom. Loosen the omelette from the side to side, so the liquid mixture flows underneath. Continue until all the liquid is lightly set.
Fold or roll away from the handle. Tip on to a hot dish and serve at once.

Soufflé omelette

cooking time : few minutes
cooking appliances : boiling ring and grill

you will need for 1 serving :

2 eggs	seasoning*
1 tablespoon water	¾ oz. butter
* or sugar, see recipes on page 84.	

1 Separate the egg yolks and the whites.
2 Whisk the yolks with the water and seasoning or sugar (many soufflé omelettes are served as a dessert, see page 84).
3 Whisk the egg whites until very stiff and fold into the yolk mixture.
4 Heat the butter in the omelette pan, pour in the egg mixture and cook until set on the bottom.
5 The mixture will still be very soft on top, so put

the omelette pan under a moderately hot grill for a few minutes to set. Fold or fill and fold as an ordinary omelette.

Note:

If you have no grill then you must cook sufficiently slowly so that the omelette becomes cooked on top without being over-cooked on the base.

Fillings for omelettes

If you have just one boiling pan it is better to make the filling first if it needs to be cooked and to keep this hot in the pan while you make the omelette. In this way you prevent over-cooking the eggs.

Some savoury fillings for omelettes

These are generally put into a plain omelette, but there is no reason why they cannot be used with a savoury soufflé omelette if wished. The fillings are enough for 1 person.

Asparagus omelette: fill the omelette with hot canned or cooked asparagus, or a tin of concentrated asparagus soup.

Bacon omelette: fry diced bacon in the omelette pan, add a little butter when the bacon is cooked and heat. Pour in the eggs and cook in the usual way.

Bread omelette: this makes an omelette just a little more substantial. Use 1½ oz. butter. Dice a slice of bread, removing the crusts. Cook in the hot butter until golden brown on both sides, add the eggs and continue as before. Fill with sliced tomato or other cooked vegetables before folding. This is not suitable for a soufflé type of omelette as you have a very firm crisp crust.

Cheese omelette: fill the omelette with 1–2 oz. grated cheese, cottage or cream cheese. Sliced uncooked tomato may be added if wished.

Ham omelette: add 1–2 oz. finely chopped, cooked ham to the eggs before cooking. Salami or other cooked meats may be used.

Herb omelette: add a good pinch dried herbs, or about 1 teaspoon chopped fresh herbs to the beaten eggs before cooking.

Mushroom omelette: heat 1 oz. butter in the pan, cook 2 oz. sliced mushrooms until tender.

Add to the beaten eggs, then heat another ½–¾ oz. butter in pan and proceed as before.

Prawn omelette: toss about 2 oz. canned or defrosted frozen prawns in about 1 tablespoon cream from the top of the milk. Fill the omelette with this mixture just before serving.

Spanish omelette: this is an excellent omelette to plan with left-over vegetables, cooked meat, cooked or shell-fish or a mixture of these. Heat the vegetables, fish or meat in butter or oil until very hot. Tip out of the pan into the beaten eggs. Add a little more butter to the pan, cook the omelette in the usual way but do not fold before serving.

Tomato omelette: either fill the omelette with sliced raw tomatoes, cooked tomatoes or concentrated tomato soup.

Easy soufflés

A soufflé is generally made with a thick white sauce, etc., but since this generally makes too much for one person I have tried this method with potato for savoury soufflés, with great success.

Basic savoury soufflé

cooking time: 20 minutes
cooking appliances: boiling ring and
oven

you will need for 1 serving:

1 tablespoon dehydrated potato	seasoning
	flavouring, see below
¼ pint milk	2 eggs
½ oz. butter	

1 Put the potato powder into the warmed milk in a saucepan, add the butter, seasoning and flavouring.
2 Separate the egg whites from the yolks, add the yolks to the potato mixture.
3 Whisk the egg whites until very stiff, then fold into the potato mixture with a metal spoon, do this carefully so the mixture is very light.
4 Bake for approximately 18 minutes in the centre of a moderate oven (375°F., Gas Mark 4–5) until just set, then serve at once.

Flavourings

Asparagus: add about 3 tablespoons chopped, canned asparagus or use ordinary (not condensed) asparagus soup instead of milk. Other vegetable soups can be used.

Cheese: add 1½ oz. grated cheese at stage 2

after the egg yolks.

Spinach: add 3 tablespoons cooked spinach to the mixture before the egg whites.

Cooking with cheese

Cheese is one of the most concentrated forms of protein or body building foods. It is equally good cooked or uncooked. It provides the basis of easy meals, a means of flavouring and adding goodness to dishes that might be lacking in taste. Buy and store cheese carefully and none need be wasted.

Hard cheeses

Fairly mild flavours which please most people are Caerphilly – the Welsh cheese, Cheshire, Cheddar, Derby, Double Gloucester, the Dutch cheeses (Edam with the red skin, Gouda with cream), Lancashire and Leicester.

The very strongly flavoured cheeses are Gorgonzola with the blue/green veins. Gruyère and Emmenthal (the continental cheese that cooks well) recognised by the holes in them. Stilton with blue veins and Parmesan, which is strongly flavoured and suitable for cooking. It can be obtained ready grated.

Grating cheese

Cheese is easier to grate when fairly dry. If fresh and crumbly it breaks badly and becomes sticky with an ordinary grater–a mouli-grater is more successful. Try therefore to leave very fresh cheese in the air to dry out. Put into the mouli-grater or rub against the grater; for sauces, e.g. Welsh Rarebit, you need not use finest side, but if adding cheese to pastry it is better to grate finely or put the cheese into an electric blender. Left-over pieces of cheese store far better if grated. Put into covered jars and keep in a cool place.

Soft cheeses

There are many soft cheeses but the following are the most popular: Bel Paese – very creamy and mild, Brie and Camembert – creamy, yet with distinct flavour when ripe, real cream cheeses – soft and mild and to be stored

carefully, cottage cheese – white and creamy and low in calories, Demi-Sel – a pasteurised cheese with 'bite'.

Processed cheeses

They are treated to make them store well. There are various mild flavours and are ideal for sandwiches.

Buying cheese

Buy cheese where the shop has a fast moving trade, so that you know you are buying good fresh cheese.

Hard cheese: should look firm but not dry on the outside. It should never be damp or show signs of mildew. Cheese which looks very crumbly in the piece is often immature and lacking in full flavour.

Soft cheese: should be just 'ripe'. If you press soft cheese like Brie and Camembert, it should yield to your touch. If there is a rather strong smell almost of ammonia, the cheese is over-ripe and should not be bought.

Do not buy vast quantities of cheese for small households—it is better to shop more often.

Buying small quantities of cheese

Cottage cheese is sold in 4 oz. cartons upwards. Because it is light in texture you can probably use the 4 oz. at one meal with other ingredients. Cream cheese or cream cheese spread is often sold in 2 oz. portions. Because it is rich in flavour and a filling texture, 2 oz. will probably suffice for a meal with other ingredients. Cheddar and other cheese is generally sold by weight. Good shops will cut off 2–3 oz. for you.

Storing cheese

Hard and processed cheeses – Cheddar, Lancashire, etc., *can* be stored in refrigerator. It must, however, be put as far away from the freezing compartment as possible to prevent it becoming too hard and losing taste and moistness. In many cabinets there is a special cheese compartment, otherwise wrap the cheese in polythene, foil or put into a closed polythene container.

Soft cheese – Brie, Camembert, should be kept at room temperature, otherwise they dry and lose so much flavour. If you need to put them in a refrigerator (to save wastage), bring out 2–3 hours before serving.

Storing cheese in your 'bedsitter'

The two former paragraphs deal with the way to store cheese if you have good facilities. In one room, cheese is not easy to store as it has such a pronounced smell, and your room is likely to be fairly warm.

Buy small portions of cheese only. If you use Cheddar or Gruyère cheese in cooking, grate this and keep it in small polythene boxes or screw-topped jars so you 'seal in' the smell. Many large grocers or supermarkets sell ready-grated cheese by weight, or Parmesan cheese is sold in drums or sealed packets.

Uncooked snacks and meals with cheese

Cheese salads

Cheese is included in some of the salads in the chapter beginning page 71 but here are some quick and easy salads based on cheese. All quantities are for one person.

With eggs

Scrambled cheese salad: scramble 1 egg in ½ oz. butter until half set. Remove from heat and blend in 2 oz. grated Cheddar cheese or diced Cheddar cheese and 1 tablespoon mayonnaise. Cool, then pile on to lettuce or watercress.

Egg and cheese salad: hard-boil and halve 1 egg. Top each half an egg with 1 oz. cream cheese and a gherkin. Serve on sliced tomatoes.

With fruit

Fill 2 peach or pear halves (canned or fresh) with either 2 oz. cream cheese or 4 oz. cottage cheese. Serve with watercress. The stronger Danish Blue cheese also blends with fruit.

Cut a dessert apple in slices, spread with a little mayonnaise and top with cream or cottage cheese and dates, raisins, nuts. Serve with segments of orange and watercress.

With vegetables

Cheese blends with most salad ingredients. Either dice or grate hard cheeses or use the soft cheese.

With meat or fish

If you have a small quantity of canned or cooked meat or fish left, it will be enough for a meal if diced and mixed with diced cheese. Here are some interesting blendings of flavours:

With meat

Beef and Stilton or Danish Blue.

Fried bacon, chopped when crisp, mixed with diced Danish Blue or Gouda cheese.

Cooked ham with diced Gruyère.

Canned luncheon meat with crumbled Lancashire.

Cooked sausages, diced and mixed with diced Cheddar cheese and a little chutney.

With fish

Anchovy fillets and Cheddar cheese.

Tuna and cottage cheese.

Salmon and grated Cheddar or Gruyère.

Cheese fingers

Cut fingers of fresh bread (without crusts). Spread with cream or cottage cheese and roll in cornflakes.

Open sandwiches

Place sliced cheese on bread and butter or buttered crispbread and top with fruit, sliced tomato, chutney, mustard pickle, etc.

Hints on cooking with cheese

Cheddar, Cheshire, Emmanthal, Lancashire, Dutch, Gruyère and Parmesan cheeses are excellent for cooking purposes, either sliced, diced or grated. Never over-cook cheese otherwise it becomes tough and stringy. If you are adding cheese to a sauce, thicken this first THEN add the cheese.

If a dish containing cheese is to be put in the oven, make sure you time the cooking time correctly. If it has to be kept waiting for a time, lower heat to prevent over-cooking.

With grilled cheese or cheese 'toppings' that are

put under a grill, pre-heat the grill first so cheese melts and browns in shortest possible time.

Cooked snacks with cheese

Serve these with watercress or other green vegetables or salad.

Baked cheese

Cover a buttered oven-proof plate with several thick slices of Cheddar cheese. Top with a little butter and bake for 10 minutes towards the top of a moderately hot oven. (375–400°F., Gas Mark 5–6).

To vary:
With tomato: put thick slices of tomato below and above the cheese.
With potato: put thin slices of canned or cooked potato below and above the cheese.
With egg: break 1 or 2 eggs on top of the cheese, add a little butter on top of the eggs and set the eggs and bake the cheese together.

Cheese and vegetable bake

Heat a small can of mixed vegetables or baked beans in a saucepan, tip into a dish, top with sliced or grated cheese and bake in the oven as above.

Fried cheese

Put fairly thick slices of Cheddar, Gruyère or Cheshire cheese into a well-greased, heated frying pan and cook for 3 minutes. Serve with tomatoes or add the cheese after frying bacon – the two are delicious together.

Grilled or toasted cheese

Sliced or grated cheese can help to provide a variety of dishes that are grilled.

Toasted cheese

Top buttered toast with a good layer of grated Cheddar, Gruyère, Cheshire, Double Gloucester, Gouda or processed cheese and heat under the grill, or use a thick slice of cheese instead.

Ham and cheese toast

Put a slice of cooked ham on buttered toast, spread with mustard or chutney and the cheese and heat under the grill.

Vegetable toasts

Put heated vegetables in a dish or on toast, and top with the cheese and cook as above.

Celery and cheese toast

Put a heated canned celery heart (well-drained) on hot buttered toast. Top with cheese and cook as above.

Sardine and cheese toast

Mash sardines on to hot buttered toast, top with a sliced tomato. Heat for 1–2 minutes under the grill, then add the top layer of cheese and reheat under grill.

Cheese custard

cooking time: 40 minutes
cooking appliance: oven

you will need for 1 serving:

1 egg	2 oz. Cheddar or
½ pint milk	1 oz. Parmesan cheese
seasoning	

to garnish:
1 tomato or little parsley or cress

1 Beat the egg, add the milk, seasoning and grated cheese.
2 Put into an oven-proof dish and bake in the centre of a very moderate oven (325–350°F., Gas Mark 3–4) until set.
3 Top with sliced tomato or other garnish. Serve hot or cold.

To vary:
Bacon and cheese custard: fry 1 rasher bacon, chop, put into dish, add the mixture above and cook as basic recipe.
Fish and cheese custard: put 1 small fillet fish (uncooked) in the dish, add the mixture above and cook as basic recipe.
Vegetable and cheese custard: put cooked or canned sliced potatoes, carrots or mixed vegetables into the dish. Heat for about 10 minutes, add the custard and cook as above.
Savoury bread and butter pudding: put 1 slice

buttered bread, cut into neat fingers, in the dish, add the mixture above and cook as basic recipe.

Cooked vegetables and cheese

Most vegetables blend well with cheese. See under vegetable dishes, commencing on page 63.

Cheese and pasta

Cheese is a natural accompaniment to spaghetti etc. See under pasta dishes, commencing on page 72.

Cheese and rice

Many savoury rice dishes, commencing on page 76, blend well with cheese.

Cooking with fish

Fish is a protein food that cooks quickly, is easily digested and can be served in a great variety of ways. It has the great disadvantage though that it has such a definite smell and this can be very unpleasant in a restricted living space. In many of the recipes therefore I have given canned fish (tuna or salmon, etc.) as an alternative since these do not smell as strongly as fresh fish, so you may prefer to use these. Wrapping fish in foil is another way to reduce the smell of cooking fish, see various recipes. If you can buy fish at a time when the fishmonger is not too busy, he will probably be willing to skin, fillet or prepare fish for you.

Choosing fresh fish

Take care in buying fish. If you shop on your way to work it is unwise to keep fish in your shopping basket all day, as it deteriorates so quickly. This is why frozen fish, which keeps frozen for some hours, is often a better purchase.

Choosing white fish

There is a great variety in white fish, many more than I have given, so look critically round your fishmonger's shop. White fish should look firm and white, with a pleasant smell NEVER BUY THIS IF IT SMELLS OF AMMONIA.

These are the white fish you will find most of the year in your fishmongers:

Cod – you can buy either a small part of a fillet (4–6 oz. is an average portion) or 1 cod steak (often called a cutlet). As a cutlet contains a bone as well as skin, allow 6–8 oz. for an average portion. Cod has a very definite flavour and is excellent in 'made-up' fish dishes as well as cooked by the usual methods – grilling, frying, etc.

Fresh haddock – buy as cod; fresh haddock has a finer texture and a more delicate flavour than cod.

Hake – buy as cod; hake is less strong than cod.

Halibut or turbot – these are both white fish that are expensive but very filling and a wonderful buy for special occasions. You buy both these fish in slices (cutlets or steaks) and 4–6 oz. give a medium portion.

Plaice – one of the most delicious of white fish when at its best. In Spring in Britain it tends to produce large roes and be somewhat watery in texture. Buy a large or two small fillets for a good portion 5–6 oz., or a small whole fish (get the fishmonger to remove the head for you).

Plaice can be cooked in all the usual ways – grilled, fried, etc.

Sole – buy as plaice. It is admirable in 'made-up' dishes but more expensive. There are various types of sole, e.g., Dover, lemon, witch, dab.

Whiting – a small delicately flavoured and easily digested white fish, which can be cut into fillets and cooked as plaice or cooked whole.

Frozen white fish

Cod, fresh haddock, plaice are some of the white fish that may be purchased ready frozen. It is possible to purchase the frozen fish with a coating of egg and crumb or fish fingers made from white fish.

Follow the directions on the packet regarding defrosting. Some fish is cooked from the frozen state.

White fish does not can well.

Choosing smoked fish

Some smoked fish is often served as an hors d'oeuvre – see page 13, but smoked fish as below make a main dish.

Cod and haddock – either smoked as fillet in which case allow about 6–8 oz. per person or as whole fish.

It may be a little difficult to buy a sufficiently small fish for one person, but occasionally you will see small fish often called "Smokies". Smoked haddock often called Finnan Haddock is excellent for breakfast or a main dish. The most usual method of cooking is by poaching, see page 32.

Kippers and bloaters – cured herrings can be cooked by various methods. They do have a very pronounced smell though and so they are better if 'jugged' as page 32 or baked as page 32.

Buy 1 large or 2 small kippers or bloaters.

Frozen smoked fish

Smoked haddock and kippers are sold in polythene bags and you can 'boil in the bag', so retaining flavour and reducing smell.

The smoked fish above is not canned.

Choosing shellfish

Many shellfish are sold ready cooked, e.g. lobster, crab, prawns, making them ideal for quick meals. They are expensive fish and it is important to buy a sufficiently small amount so it may be eaten while fresh. All fish is dangerous to eat when stale, shellfish particularly.

Crab – the claws of crab should be firm looking. A good crab feels heavy for its size, if light it denotes it is rather 'watery'. Buy a small crab per person for a main dish or 4 oz. crab meat, which is often sold by weight. In a salad you have a more interesting flavour if you use light and dark meat. To prepare crab salad, page 39. See also canned and frozen crab.

Lobster – this is fresh if bright red; the tail springs back into position when pulled hard; the comment about weight given under the crab also applies to the lobster. There are quite a number of lobster dishes in this book for special occasions.

Buy 1 small lobster per person for a main dish or allow ½ medium sized lobster. To prepare, see lobster salad. See also canned lobster and frozen lobster.

Mussels – these make a first class meal, see moules marinière below.

They should be firm with bright looking shells. Unfortunately it is not easy to judge mussels until you get them home, you must just rely on having a good fishmonger. If you DO find they are stale, they should be returned to the shop.

Allow 1–1½ pints per person.

To open mussels, scrub well and remove beard, discard any that do not close when the shell is tapped hard. Put into a saucepan with dehydrated onion, or a chopped onion, about ½ pint cold water, seasoning and a bunch parsley. Heat for about 5–7 minutes until the shells open.

Serve the mussels in the liquid. This is a simple recipe for **moules marinière**.

Prawns and shrimps – they should be bright and firm as stated under lobster. If buying fish *in* shells you need approximately 1 pint. See also canned and frozen prawns and canned shrimps.

Scallops or escallops – these are an excellent purchase for one person as you buy them singly. They are easy to prepare and not unduly expensive. Scallops are sold in their shells – ask the fishmonger for the shell if you need it for serving the scallops. These fish are fresh if the flesh looks firm and white and the roe is a clear bright orange. Scallops are sold uncooked. Allow 1 large scallop per person.

There are other shellfish ranging from the lordly oyster to the humble cockle but these are less valuable in providing quick dishes.

Frozen shellfish

A selection of shellfish is frozen today. Always allow frozen shellfish to thaw out gradually before using.

Crab – this is very good indeed in salads or cooked dishes. Allow the same quantity as when fresh. Frozen crab meat is sold off the shell and so it is particularly suitable when you have little space for preparation.

Lobster – these are somewhat rare. At the moment the only frozen lobsters are in their shells so you allow the lobster to thaw out and prepare it as fresh.

Prawns – one of the most usual frozen fish. While you can buy frozen prawns *in* their shells, most fishmongers sell them ready shelled. Allow 2 oz. for a small portion as a main dish. Tiny shrimps are not available in this form.

Scampi – the popular and accepted name for very large prawn or tails of langoustine (like tiny lobster). Although expensive, you can buy very excellent uncooked shelled scampi in the frozen state.

Scallops – a few fishmongers sell home frozen scallops but these are a rarity.

To hasten defrosting of frozen shellfish, put the wrapped fish in cold water. If you put it into hot water to defrost, you toughen the fish.

Canned shellfish

Lobster and crab meat are expensive when canned but retain their flavour well.

Mussels are sold in cans or jars out of their shells and are ready cooked. They are of a good flavour.

Prawns and shrimps also can well. Although they have a softer texture than fresh or frozen prawns, the canned variety taste very good.

Potted shrimps – these are shrimps cooked, shelled and blended with flavoured butter. Although generally served as an hors d'oeuvre with lettuce, lemon and bread and butter or toast and butter, they can form a light main dish, see page 43.

The small carton filled with the potted shrimps thaws out very quickly, so you can serve this within 30 minutes of the shop assistant taking it from the deep freeze.

Choosing oily fish

This is the group of fish rich in natural oils which gives additional fat, vitamins and protein, in the diet. These fish have a pronounced flavour and fairly strong smell, so special care should be taken to cook the fish in such a way that you minimise this.

The most useful and usual oily fish to buy and cook by simple means are:

Herring – one of the cheapest of foods you can buy as well as being highly nutritious. Herrings are fresh when they look firm with a bright silver skin and bright eyes. Ask the fishmonger to clean the herring and remove the head. He may also ask if you would like it filleted and this is suitable for all recipes *in this book* and will save you over-handling the fish.

Allow 1 medium to large herring per person.

Mackerel – select as herring. As a larger fish though, you will find 1 small to medium mackerel sufficient for one person.

Salmon and salmon trout – the latter is always cheaper, but most people agree the flavour is NOT as fine as real salmon.

The skin of real salmon should be bright and silver and the flesh should be firm and pink. Salmon is very filling so a slice of about 4–6oz. gives a good portion for one person. The slice is often described as a steak or cutlet.

Sprats – these tiny inexpensive fish are delicious. Choose as herring. Allow 8 oz. for one person.

Frozen oily fish

Frozen or chilled **salmon** is brought into this country when fresh salmon is not available, it is generally cheaper than the fresh fish. Fishmongers generally defrost the salmon so they cut it into desired portions. It does tend to be less moist than fresh salmon.

Canned oily fish

Both **tuna** (a fish not obtainable fresh in this country) and **salmon** are very popular. The fish is ready to serve if required or can be used in hot dishes. If cooking with canned salmon you can economise if you buy pink salmon; the red salmon is better in salads. There are small cans available, the problem with many canned fish is that the can tends to be too large for one.

Anchovies are oily fish which are found fresh in Italy but canned in this country. They serve as a flavouring rather than a main dish since the canned variety are very salty.

Brisling are like sardines.

Herrings, canned in tomato sauce, are ready to serve and very good in salads or in cooked dishes. Rollmop herrings are often sold individually in delicatessen shops or in jars, they are ready to serve.

Bismarck herrings are sold in jars and as they are pickled they keep well for several days in a cool place, when once the jar is opened. Scandinavian herring 'tit-bits' are excellent for snacks at a party. You buy these in small tins and serve them with or on bread and butter.

Pilchards are delicious fish and do not often appear in fishmongers away from Cornwall, where they are caught. They are plentiful in canned form, use as canned herrings, page 44.

Sardines in the fresh state are used in Portuguese cooking as they are in abundance there. Canned in oil or tomato sauce, they are ideal for salads and in snacks, see pages 28 and 71.

Choosing freshwater fish

Freshwater fish is the term used to describe the fish caught in lakes, streams, etc. Few are sold by fishmongers, except trout, which is an excellent main dish.

Frozen freshwater fish

Frozen trout is fairly easy to obtain in good stores. Often called 'Rainbow trout'; you can cook this from the frozen state. You may need to buy 2 trout at one time. These are not obtainable in canned form.

Choosing fish roes

The roes of fish are sold separately from the fish. They are easy to digest and comparatively inexpensive to buy.

The one exception costwise is caviare. True caviare (from Russia) comes from sturgeon and is very costly but you can buy much cheaper caviare today (often from Denmark). It is generally served as an hors d'oeuvre on lettuce with lemon, toast and butter. Caviare is ready to serve.

Other roes obtainable are:

Cod roe – you may find this uncooked, in which case follow directions on page 38. Allow 5–6 oz. per person. Try to buy the cooked cod's roe as this saves you time.

There are many ways in which you can serve the roe as pages 38–39. Allow 3–4 oz. per person.

Smoked cod roe – this is pink in colour and very salty in flavour. It is served as hors d'oeuvre with toast and butter, lemon and lettuce – when mixed with other ingredients it forms an excellent pâté, as page 39.

Herring roe – the roes one generally buys are soft herring roes – although sometimes hard roes are obtainable. Both of these are excellent for light dishes, see page 44. Allow 4 oz. per person.

Canned roes

Caviare is sold in small jars.

Herring roes are sold in cans, generally enough for two or more people though. Canning softens the roes, so they need little heating.

Basic recipes with fish

This section gives you many easy recipes using fish of all kinds.

There are basic ways of cooking fish and since these are referred to in the recipes, it is advisable to read them firstly. Wash the fish in cold water then dry on a piece of kitchen paper.

Boiling or poaching fish

The term boiling is often used to describe this method of cooking, but fish should NOT be cooked in boiling liquid since it destroys much of the flavour of the fish and is inclined to break it too. Instead the fish should be simmered gently, hence the name 'poaching'.

The liquid used can be water but individual recipes give other suggestions.

Timing – this is given in the recipes but if you put the fish into cold liquid (enough to cover) and bring this just to simmering point you would allow:

3–4 minutes for fillets of fish

5–7 minutes for cutlets of fish

about 10 minutes for whole small fish. This method however gives a strong smell of cooking, so you will see I advocate wrapping the fish in foil which means an extra 5–8 minutes cooking time.

Baking fish

If you have an oven, this is probably the best way to cook the fish, for the smell is very faint. You can wrap the fish in foil or cover the cooking dish tightly so you keep in all the flavour and most of the odour. The covering can be a lid, foil, potato, pastry, etc. Since recipes vary a great deal, times are given under each dish.

Roasting fish

This means the fish is cooked in fat in the oven, rather like a joint of meat; see various recipes on pages 36 to 42.

Fish in a casserole

There are a number of fish casseroles and stews in this book. Some of the most interesting are on page 40.

Frying fish

As pans of deep fat or oil are difficult to keep in a tiny kitchen, I have only described shallow frying.

To minimise the smell use a frying pan with a lid where possible, or cover the pan with foil. This does prevent the fish becoming as crisp as one would wish. The fish is often first coated with seasoned flour or egg and crumbs or milk and crumbs – see below, then fried in hot fat.

To coat fish in flour or cornflour

For 1 fillet or cutlet of fish allow 2 level teaspoons flour or cornflour, plus a good pinch of salt and shake of pepper.

Put the seasoned flour or cornflour on to a plate or into a paper bag. Press the well-dried fish into the flour on the plate, turn and coat on the second side *or* drop the fish into the bag and shake gently until the fish is coated.

Egg and crumb coating

For 1 medium fillet or cutlet of fish, you need about ¼ of an egg or use part of the white only and save the rest of the egg for another recipe, or brush the fish with milk instead of egg. Put about half the egg white on to a plate or use the whole white or the whole yolk or ½ the beaten egg for 2 medium fillets.

Dip the fish first on one side then on the other side in the egg (or use 2 teaspoons cream from the top of the milk instead). If you have a pastry brush then brush each side of the fish with the egg or milk. Put ½ tablespoon crisp breadcrumbs on to a plate. Put the fish on to these on the plate, press against the crumbs so they 'stick' well then turn and repeat on the second side, or put the crumbs into a paper bag, drop in the fish and shake until coated.

Always press the crumbs against the fish with a flat knife before frying to make sure they do not fall off during cooking.

To fry: heat approximately 1 oz. fat in a frying pan or use ½ oz. only with a silicone (non-stick) pan. Heat the fat until melted. Put in the fish, fry steadily on the under side until golden coloured, turn with a fish slice or wide bladed palette knife and cook on the second side.

Timing: thin fillets take about 2 minutes on either side; thicker cutlets (slices) about 4–5 minutes on either side, so it is wise to turn the heat down after frying 2–3 minutes on either side. Whole fish takes 10–12 minutes in all.

To make sure the fish is not 'soggy' put on a piece of kitchen roll on a plate or tin for 1 minute. The paper absorbs any surplus fat.

Ready coated fish

There is a very time saving development in frozen fish, in that this may now be obtained already coated with egg and crumbs. If the quantity is not too large or you have a refrigerator to store the surplus, it is worthwhile buying this type of fish. You do not need to wait for the fish to defrost. The cooking time is almost the same as fresh fish and is given on the packets.

Oven 'fried' fish

In this method the fish is coated as above and put on to a *heated* tin or oven-proof plate, which should have been brushed with a few drops of oil or about ¼ oz. melted fat, butter or margarine.

Top the fish with a few drops of oil or ¼ oz. melted fat, butter or margarine and put the fish towards the top of a moderately hot to hot oven (400–425°F., Gas Mark 5–6). Allow 10–12 minutes for fillets and 15–20 minutes for cutlets and a little longer for whole fish.

Grilling fish

Cover the grid of the grill pan with a piece of foil. You can wash and use this again or discard it after the fish is cooked. In either case, you have less smell as this tends to cling to the metal grill pan grid.

To grill

Spread the piece of foil with $\frac{1}{4}$–$\frac{1}{2}$ oz. butter or margarine. If not using foil, brush the grid of the grill pan with the butter or margarine. Put the seasoned fish on top, with any flavourings suggested in the recipes and any butter or margarine. Heat the grill and cook the fish. The times are the same as for frying, page 33. Thin fillets do not need turning.

Steaming fish

This method is generally recommended for invalids, but since it is so simple I feel it an invaluable method to use in a 'bedsitter'. Normally, the fish is put on one plate with a little butter, milk and seasoning or any other flavourings given in the recipe and covered with a second plate or saucepan lid. This is placed over a pan of steadily boiling water and since the plate covers the pan effectively you will have very little steam in the room.

Timing: allow 5–6 minutes for thin fillets, 8–10 minutes for cutlets of fish. Whole fish is rarely cooked in this manner.

Some flavourings for fish dishes

Fish often *needs* extra flavouring and here are some useful 'stand-bys'.

Mayonnaise or salad dressing: instead of making a sauce you can use the commercially prepared products which keep well in their screw-topped jars.

Canned soups: these can also be used as sauces – see the recipes.

Fish pastes: tiny jars are excellent as an instant 'stuffing' for fish. When once the jar is opened the contents must be used at once.

In addition, consider some of these:

Capers: these keep well in their jars even when opened. Make certain you do not tip out the vinegar from the jar which acts as a preservative.

Gherkins: these take the place of cucumber in many dishes, bottled gherkins keep well, see under 'capers' for comments.

Herbs: thyme, parsley, fennel in particular blend with fish. Drums of dried herbs keep indefinitely.

Lemon: flavouring is almost a 'must' with fish. If you feel that part of a fresh lemon could be wasted, buy a plastic lemon (you can squeeze out a few drops) or use the bottled lemon juice.

Tomato: use either fresh or canned tomatoes or tomato ketchup. The concentrated tomato purée, sold in cans or tubes, is excellent with meat or poultry but can be a little strong with fish.

You will find almonds, beetroot, celery, cheese, dates, eggs, peppers, paprika, all add interesting flavours to fish.

Recipes using fish

Note:

Some of the recipes are based on classic dishes e.g. trout with almonds, sole with grapes, but since the method of making is NOT entirely classic I have avoided the proper name in the title, but indicated this in the recipe.

All quantities are for one person unless stated to the contrary and the fish are given alphabetically.

Using anchovy fillets

Use $\frac{1}{2}$ small can anchovies for each dish. Left over anchovies may be used also in: stuffed potato, page 70 and tomato salad, page 13.

Anchovy tomato bake

cooking appliance: oven

Slice 2 tomatoes, blend with chopped anchovy fillets and shake pepper. Put into small oven-proof dish. Top with 1 or 2 beaten and seasoned eggs and bake for 15 minutes towards top of moderate to moderately hot oven (375–400°F., Gas Mark 4–5).

Anchovy and potato au gratin

cooking appliance: oven

1 Slice 3–4 medium cooked or 6 small canned potatoes and put into an oven-proof dish.
2 Add chopped anchovies and grated Cheddar cheese to each layer of potato.

Top this with 1 egg beaten with 1 tablespoon cream from the top of the milk, seasoning and ½ oz. grated cheese. Bake for 20 minutes in a very moderate to moderate oven (350–375°F., Gas Mark 3–4).

Any left-over potatoes may be used in potato salads, page 72, or sauté potatoes, page 70.

Buckling and bloaters

Both these fish are excellent in various ways. The former can be served without cooking if required, but can be cooked as bloaters *or* follow directions for smoked trout on page 49.

Baked buckling or bloater

cooking time: 15-25 minutes
cooking appliance: oven

you will need for 1 serving:

1 bloater or buckling   pepper
½ oz. margarine or butter   squeeze lemon juice

to garnish:

watercress

1 Remove the head, if not already done. Split the fish and take out the backbone – see page 42 under boning herrings.
2 Spread margarine or butter over a piece of foil or greaseproof paper.
3 Put the fish on this, add a shake of pepper and squeeze of lemon juice.
4 Wrap up the fish neatly, put on to an ovenproof plate or tin (this prevents any oil from fish seeping into the oven should the foil or paper not be sealed firmly).
5 Bake towards the top of a moderately hot oven (375–400°F., Gas Mark 4–5) for 15–20 minutes for buckling or 20–25 minutes for bloaters.
6 Garnish with watercress.

To vary:

Although greaseproof paper could be used for these variations, the other ingredients make a very heavy 'parcel' so it is advisable to use foil or to put the ingredients on to an oven-proof plate or dish.

Baked with tomatoes, capers and parsley: cover the buttered foil, plate or dish with 1 or 2 thickly sliced tomatoes, season lightly. Add ½ teaspoon capers, and/or a pinch of dried parsley or ½ teaspoon chopped fresh parsley. Put the fish on top of this, wrap firmly in the foil, or cover the plate or dish with greased greaseproof paper.
Bake as above.

If wished the plate or dish may be left uncovered, but this is inclined to let the tomatoes dry out a little and it does produce a far stronger smell in the room.

With onions and tomatoes: put 1 teaspoon dehydrated onion in ⅓ tablespoon water for 10 minutes, then blend with the tomatoes in the recipe above or use a very tiny fresh onion and chop or grate this finely.

Fried buckling

Heat for a very few minutes in a little hot fat and serve with fried almonds or fried parsley as trout, page 48.

Fried bloater

Fry in fat as described on page 33 for a total of 7–8 minutes.
To give extra flavour, fry sliced mushrooms in the fat at the same time as the fish.

Grilled buckling or bloater

cooking appliance: grill

Prepare grill as page 33.

Heat the grill very thoroughly if cooking the buckling, as it is already cooked and needs heating on either side only.

Brush the buckling or bloater with very little butter, add pepper, squeeze of lemon if you wish. Cook buckling for about 1½–2 minutes, turn and cook on the second side for 1½–2 minutes. Bloaters need 4–5 minutes on either side.

To vary:

With lemon flavour: grate the rind of ½–1 lemon over the fish before cooking and after you have brushed it with butter. Press this rind firmly against the fish.

With tomato coating: cover with sliced tomatoes on the second side after cooking on one side. Cook as before, but allow an extra minute or two for the heat to penetrate through the tomatoes to the fish.

Savoury buckling salad

cooking time : 10 minutes
cooking appliance : boiling ring

you will need for 1 serving :

1 egg	mayonnaise
1 buckling	½ teaspoon capers
1 dessert apple	lettuce leaves

1 Hard-boil the egg, then shell and dice while still warm.
2 Cut the flesh of the buckling into pieces, mix with the egg, the peeled, chopped apple, a little mayonnaise and capers.
3 Pile on to the lettuce leaves.

Note :

See page 68 for storing any lettuce left.

Cod

Cod is one of the most versatile fish. As well as these recipes you can use cod in the recipes for most other fish.

Baked cod

cooking appliance : oven

Cod is one of the fish that because of its moist texture and definite flavour, can be baked without extra ingredients as instructions on page 32.
On the other hand, it blends well with many other ingredients, so here are some newer ideas.

Bacon and cod

cooking appliance : oven

Put the lightly seasoned piece of cod on to an oven-proof plate or piece of foil. DO NOT grease as the bacon is fat.
Cut the rind from a rasher of streaky or back bacon, halve the bacon rasher and put over the cod.
In order to crisp the bacon do not cover.
Bake for 15–20 minutes just above the centre of a moderately hot to hot oven (400–425°F., Gas Mark 5–6).

To vary :

With tomato : put sliced tomato over the fish and under the bacon or top with tomato and omit bacon.

With potato or onion : put a layer of peeled, grated, raw, seasoned potato *under* the cod; this delays cooking so allow about 35–40 minutes in a moderate oven. A thinly sliced onion can be mixed with the potato or used instead of the potato.

Baked cod in milk

cooking appliance : oven

Put the cod into an oven-proof dish or in an oven-proof deep plate (an oven-proof soup plate is excellent for this).
Add 2–3 tablespoons milk, ½ oz. butter or margarine and a good pinch of salt and shake of pepper.
Cover with foil, greaseproof paper or a sauce-pan lid to keep the liquid from evaporating. Cook for 20–25 minutes in the centre of a moderate to moderately hot oven (375–400°F., Gas Mark 4–5).
Serve with the milk as a sauce.

To flavour :

With lemon : add a few strips of lemon rind (do not use the juice it would curdle the milk).

With parsley : add a little chopped parsley.

With mayonnaise : blend 1 tablespoon mayonnaise with 2 tablespoons milk (for a more savoury sauce) and pour this over the fish before cooking.

With cream : use thin cream or cream from the top of the milk in place of milk.

With wine or cider : use white wine or dry cider instead of milk. If using wine, you can add a chopped gherkin, a few capers and a skinned chopped tomato (if desired), this could not be added to milk as the milk would curdle.

Fried cod

cooking appliance : boiling ring

Cod may be fried as the directions on page 33. Because of the large flakes in cod, the fish breaks easily in cooking, so a good coating of flour or egg and crumbs is necessary. It *is* worthwhile coating in flour *and* egg and crumbs to give a very firm outside or to buy ready coated, frozen cod.
There are many variations on fried cod. In some recipes you can use *either* coated or uncoated fish, in others you have a better result if the fish is not coated. An indication is given in each recipe.

Cod in lemon butter

cooking appliance : boiling ring

Use coated or uncoated fish.

Heat 1½ oz. butter with the finely grated rind of ½–1 lemon (take the top part only called 'the zest' not the bitter white pith). Fry the fish in this as directions, page 33. When cooked add the juice of ½–1 lemon (to taste). Heat for 1 minute and serve.

Cod in orange butter : we generally associate lemon with fish, but many years ago orange was a usual accompaniment so you can use orange in place of lemon.

Cod in savoury butter : use the lemon rind as before, but blend 2 teaspoons lemon juice with 1 tablespoon tomato ketchup, 1 chopped gherkin. Add to the pan just before serving the fish and heat for 1 minute then spoon over the fish. 1 or 2 skinned, chopped tomatoes could be used instead of tomato ketchup.

Fried cod and cucumber

cooking time : 10 minutes
cooking appliance : boiling ring

you will need for 2 servings :

2 portions cod fillet or 2 cod steaks	½ small cucumber
seasoning	few drops lemon juice
2 oz. butter	

1 Dry the cod thoroughly and season well.
2 Heat the butter and fry the cod steadily on one side for 5 minutes.
3 Meanwhile peel the cucumber and cut into ¼ inch slices then cut each slice into strips, season.
4 Turn the cod and when you have done this, add the cucumber and lemon juice. Stand back slightly as you do this as there will be quite a lot of 'spluttering' as the moist vegetable goes into the pan. Continue cooking for another 5–6 minutes.
5 Lift the cod on to hot serving plates or a dish and top with the cucumber, which is a very pleasant flavour with fish.

Note :

I have given this dish for 2 portions as you may not be able to buy less than ½ cucumber; if you can buy a small portion of cucumber or can use any left on another occasion then make for one person reducing butter to a generous 1 oz. Do not coat the cod.

To vary :

With cucumber and ham : this is particularly good if the cod portions are small. Cut 1–2 oz. cooked lean ham into strips and add with the cucumber.

Other ways to vary fried cod

In all these methods it is better to use uncoated fresh or frozen fish. In each recipe the cod is fried in a little fat or butter on one side, turned over and the following flavourings etc. added, so the cod cooks on the second side while the other ingredients heat through.

With barbecued tomato sauce : pour ½ small can of tomato soup, blended with 2 teaspoons chutney and a few drops Worcestershire sauce over the fish.

Note :

Use rest of can of soup as a first course to another meal or in casserole, page 57.

Curried cod : pour ½ small can mulligatawny soup over the cod. To give a stronger flavour of curry you can blend ½–1 teaspoon curry powder with the soup before adding it to the fish. To add interest you can add 1–2 teaspoons sultanas or raisins to the soup or a little chutney for a sweeter flavour.

Grilled cod

cooking appliance : grill

Cod may be grilled as the directions on page 33. If grilling cutlets of cod, turn very carefully so they do not break, read instruction on lining grid of grill pan, brushing with fat, etc. on page 33.

To make the cod more interesting try it with one of the following:

Lemon : add a little lemon juice and grated rind to the fish with the seasoning.

Bacon : grill on one side, turn and cover with a halved rasher of bacon then grill on the second side.

Mustard : grill on one side, turn, brush with melted butter then spread with a thin coating of made English or French mustard before cooking on second side.

Cheese : grill on one side, turn, grill on the second side. Just before the fish is cooked remove from under the grill and top with a layer of grated Cheddar or Parmesan cheese or a slice of Gruyère, Cheddar or processed cheese. Return to the grill for a further 2 minutes until the cheese has melted. Do not over-cook otherwise the cheese is toughened.

Poached cod

cooking appliance : boiling ring

Cod may be poached as the basic instructions on page 32, adding seasoning, a little lemon juice or a few drops vinegar to the water. It may also be poached as follows:

Cod in cider

Put the portion of cod into a saucepan, add approximately $\frac{1}{4}$ pint dry or sweet cider. Bring the liquid to simmering point, cover the pan and simmer for 5–6 minutes.

To vary :

With cider sauce : as above, then lift the fish on to a hot plate (to heat this put over the saucepan in place of a saucepan lid). Blend 1 tablespoon mayonnaise into the hot cider. Coat the fish with this, top with capers or sliced gherkin.

With cider and vegetable medley : as cod in cider, but add 2 oz. thinly sliced mushrooms and 1 sliced tomato, plus tiny can of corn (do not use creamed corn). Cook with the fish.

White wine could be used in place of cider.

Cod may also be poached in milk and in slightly diluted asparagus, mushroom, tomato or vegetable soups.

For 1 portion of cod you need $\frac{1}{2}$ small can soup blended with 1 tablespoon milk or water. Use *ordinary* soup for this not the extra thick condensed soups. Cover the saucepan with a lid or plate as the fish cooks.

Smoked cod

Any of the recipes for smoked haddock may be used for cod.

Cod's roe

If you buy uncooked cod's roe you should cook this first before using.

To cook cod's roe

If you have a steamer put the roe in this. For 6–8 oz. roe, allow 7–8 minutes steady steaming over a pan of boiling water, season lightly. If you have no steamer, put the roe into a saucepan with about $\frac{1}{2}$ inch cold water, season lightly. Cover the pan tightly and cook for 7–8 minutes.

To use cooked cod's roe

Creamed roe

cooking time : 10 – 12 minutes
cooking appliance : boiling ring

you will need for 1 serving :

$\frac{1}{2}$ oz. butter	$\frac{1}{4}$ pint milk
1 teaspoon cornflour	4-6 oz. cooked cod's roe
	seasoning

1 Put the butter into a saucepan and heat.
2 Blend the cornflour and milk, add to the butter.
3 Bring to the boil, stir until slightly thickened.
4 Add the cod's roe, after removing the outer skin and cutting into 2–3 slices.
5 Season well and heat for 5 minutes.

To vary :

With cream : Stir 1–2 tablespoons thin cream or cream from the top of the milk into the sauce before adding the roe.

In mushroom sauce :

a use 1 oz. butter and fry 2 oz. sliced mushrooms in this before adding cornflour, milk, etc., *or*

b heat the $\frac{1}{2}$ oz. butter then add $\frac{1}{2}$ small can mushroom soup blended with 2 tablespoons cream from the top of the milk. Heat, then add the cod's roe and simmer gently for 5 minutes.

Other soups could be used instead of mushroom. The most suitable, in view of the delicate flavour of cod's roe, would be asparagus, cream of chicken or tomato soup. If using condensed soups, dilute with rather more milk or cream.

Fried cod's roe

Cod's roe is excellent fried, you just cut the cooked roe into pieces and fry in hot fat for 2–3 minutes on either side. It is particularly good fried in bacon fat or served with fried bacon; in this case, add the roe to the pan the moment the bacon starts to cook. If the bacon is fairly lean then heat about $\frac{1}{2}$ oz. fat in the pan before adding the cod's roe.

It is not essential to coat the slices of cod's roe before frying, but if dipped into seasoned flour before cooking you *do* produce a pleasant crisp brown on the outside.

Grilled cod's roe

This can be sliced, brushed with a little melted fat or butter and heated and browned under the grill, see information on grilling fish, page 33.

To vary :

a **With cheese :** heat the roe on both sides; top with a slice of Gruyère, Cheddar or processed cheese and heat for 2 minutes.

b Grill a rasher of bacon with the roe.

c Grill tomatoes and/ or mushrooms with the roe.

Smoked cod's roe

While this can be used as it is for a spread or hors d'oeuvre, it makes an excellent pâté with little trouble. This is sufficiently sustaining to make a light meal with toast, butter, a tomato and lettuce or watercress.

Cod's roe pâté

no cooking

you will need for 2 servings or 4 smaller portions for an hors d'oeuvre :

8 oz. smoked cod's roe	juice ½ lemon
2 oz. butter	pepper to taste
1 tablespoon thin cream	2 teaspoons tomato ketchup

1 Spoon the roe from the skin and blend with the other ingredients until smooth.

To vary :

You can add a crushed clove garlic or little garlic salt if wished.

If using a jar of cod's roe which is rather soft, use 1 oz. butter and ½ tablespoon cream only.

Note :

Left-over cod's roe (whether just cooked or smoked) should not be wasted, it makes an excellent sandwich spread.

Crab

To prepare a fresh crab is quite a time-consuming job, so if you can buy a ready 'dressed' crab from the fishmonger it is worth doing this. If you cannot then this is how to prepare it (this is cooked crab, of course).

1 First, cover your working surface with plenty of newspaper, so you may gather up the shell, etc. and dispose of it as quickly as possible.

2 Pull off all claws and wipe the shell.

3 Turn crab on its back and take the body from the main shell.

4 Remove and discard the stomach bag and grey fingers. These must not be eaten.

5 Take out all meat, putting dark and white into separate basins, then crack the top of the shell and remove pieces so there is a flat cavity to fill.

6 Crack claws and remove the meat, adding it to the light meat.

7 Arrange dark and light meat alternately in the shell and garnish with parsley.

Crab salad

Either serve the prepared crab on its shell with salad *or* do not put the crab meat back in the shell but arrange on lettuce with tomato salad which includes tomato, cucumber or gherkin, hard-boiled egg.

If using canned crab meat for a salad, take out of the can, tip on to a plate then remove the crab flesh from the fairly large bones. You find in the variety of crab used for canning that the bones run through the centre of the flesh.

Curried crab

no cooking

you will need for 1 serving or 2 as a light first course :

1 small crab or a can of crab meat	1 tablespoon mayonnaise
1 teaspoon curry powder	

to garnish :

small piece of cucumber or watercress

1 Prepare the crab as above.

2 Blend the curry powder and mayonnaise then stir in the crab meat.

3 Arrange on a dish with a ring of cucumber or watercress.

To vary :

Devilled crab: use a good pinch curry powder, a few drops Worcestershire sauce and ½–1 teaspoon of made English or French mustard. Add to 1 tablespoon mayonnaise.

Hot curried and devilled crab: both of these recipes are excellent for a hot crab dish. Prepare as above then either put back into the shell or into a heat-resistant dish. Top with 1 tablespoon crisp breadcrumbs and ½ oz. butter. Either heat for 5 minutes under the grill or for 10–15 minutes towards the top of a hot oven.

Curried and devilled lobster: canned, fresh or defrosted lobster may be used instead of crab in both the recipes above.

Fish cakes

The method of making fish cakes yourself is given on page 46 under salmon fish cakes, but you can buy frozen fish cakes made of white fish or salmon. One great advantage is that they are sold in small quantities. To cook these, follow the directions on the packet.

To make fish cakes more interesting:

a **With baked beans:** cook by frying, grilling or baking and top with piping hot baked beans.

b **With cheese:** grill the fish cakes. When cooked, top with a slice of processed cheese and heat for 1–2 minutes under the grill until the cheese melts.

c **With egg:** fry the fish cakes and top with a fried egg.

Fish cakes, like fish fingers, make an excellent breakfast dish.

Fish casseroles

Most white fish can be used for this type of dish, but try a firm textured white fish such as cod, hake, or for more luxurious occasions, halibut or turbot.

Two portions are given as the dish is very good cold, except where thickened soup is used, as in the variation on fish, tomato and onion casserole.

Fish casserole

cooking time: 35 minutes
cooking appliance: oven

you will need for 2 servings:

2 portions white fish (uncoated)	¼ pint white wine or cider
small can mixed vegetables	seasoning

1 Put the fish, well-drained vegetables and the wine or cider into a casserole.

2 Season lightly and cover with foil or a lid.

3 Bake for 35 minutes in the centre of a very moderate to moderate oven (350–375°F., Gas Mark 3–4).

To vary:

With frozen vegetables: if you use a small packet of mixed frozen vegetables or peas and carrots, etc., use a little less wine or cider as these are more moist than drained, canned vegetables.

Tomato casserole: omit the wine or cider and use a small can of tomatoes.

Mushroom casserole: omit the mixed vegetables, add 2 oz. sliced uncooked or canned mushrooms. Other canned vegetables such as carrots, corn, etc., may be used.

Fish, tomato and onion casserole

cooking time: approximately 40 minutes
cooking appliance: oven

you will need for 2 servings:

2 portions white fish – (uncoated)	8 oz. tomatoes
1 oz. butter	4 tablespoons water or white wine or cider
1 onion or equivalent in dehydrated onion	seasoning

1 Put the fish into the casserole.

2 Heat the butter and fry the chopped onion in this, then add the chopped tomatoes (skinned if wished), the liquid and a little seasoning.

3 Heat for about 3 minutes, until the tomatoes are slightly softened, then pour the mixture over the fish.

4 Cover the casserole with foil or a lid and bake in a very moderate to moderate oven (350–375°F, Gas Mark 3–4) for 30 minutes.

To vary:

a Omit the tomatoes and water and use a can of tomato soup or the equivalent in dehydrated soup – cooking this first as instructions given on the packet.

b Omit the onion and tomatoes and use a can of French onion soup.

c Omit the tomatoes and water and use a can of mushroom soup or the equivalent in dehydrated soup – cooking this first as instructions given on the packet.

Fish fingers

These small fingers, which you buy frozen, are made of white fish coated with egg and crumbs. Follow the directions on the packet for frying, grilling or baking. You can serve these fingers for breakfast, part of a main meal or as a light snack.

Fish fingers can be made more interesting if you:

a Serve them with a cheese sauce, page 74. This adds extra protein too.

b Twist a rasher of bacon, which has had the rind removed, round each fish finger before it is fried or grilled. Streaky bacon is a wise choice for it is economical and gives sufficient fat to keep the fish fingers moist. The bacon will also add extra protein to this dish.

Fresh haddock

Fresh haddock is an excellent fish. It is not unduly expensive to buy, has a good flavour (not quite as strong as cod) and a fine but firm texture, so it is easy to handle in cooking. Take care that haddock does not dry during cooking. The methods of cooking under cod, pages 36 to 38 and plaice, page 45, are suitable for haddock, but the following recipes are particularly good with this white fish which has a long season.

Stuffed haddock

cooking time : 20 – 25 minutes
cooking appliance : oven

you will need for 1 serving :

1 small jar fish paste (salmon, sardine etc.)	$\frac{1}{2}$-$\frac{3}{4}$ oz. margarine or butter
1 portion fresh haddock (preferably piece of fillet)	

1 Open the jar of paste and use half of this. Seal down the jar and use the remainder within a day if possible. It can be put on toast or used as a sandwich filling.

2 Make a deep cut down the centre of a piece of fillet.

3 Put the paste in this, then wrap the fish in buttered foil or put on to a buttered oven-proof plate or dish and top with buttered greaseproof paper or foil.

4 Bake for 20 minutes above the centre of a

moderate to moderately hot oven (375–400°F., Gas Mark 4–5).

To vary :

Fill the centre cavity with a few prawns or a skinned, chopped tomato.

Fill the centre cavity as above, then coat the fish with egg and crumbs and fry as page 33.

Steamed haddock

cooking time : 10 minutes
cooking appliance : boiling ring

you will need for 1 serving :

$\frac{1}{2}$ oz. butter	2 tablespoons thin cream or cream from top of the milk
1 portion haddock	seasoning

1 Spread half the butter over a plate which is strong enough to put over boiling water. Add the fish, cream, rest of the butter and seasoning.

2 Cover with a second plate, foil or a saucepan lid and stand over a saucepan of boiling water and allow the water to boil steadily for 10 minutes.

To vary :

With mayonnaise : use mayonnaise or salad cream instead of cream.

With mushrooms : add 1 or 2 oz. thinly sliced, uncooked mushrooms to the recipe.

With paprika : blend $\frac{1}{2}$ teaspoon paprika with the milk.

With tomato : use bottled or canned tomato juice in place of milk.

Smoked haddock

This is an ideal fish for breakfast, as well as for a main meal.

You may be able to buy frozen smoked haddock tightly sealed in a polythene bag, which is simply put into a pan of water and the water is allowed to simmer or boil for the time given on the packet.

If you wish to adopt this technique with the smoked haddock you buy, wrap the fish in buttered foil and tie it into a neat parcel with string. Put the parcel into the saucepan, cover with cold water and bring the water just to boiling point. Lower the heat and let the water simmer for 8–10 minutes for a thick piece of smoked haddock fillet or just about 7–8 minutes for a small, thin, whole smoked haddock with bone.

The advantage of this method is you have little smell of fish.

The disadvantage is that you have a slightly more salt flavour to the fish, so it becomes extra important to buy smoked haddock from a fishmonger where you find it mildly cured only.

Dishes with smoked haddock

Some of the variations below counteract the salt flavour of smoked haddock.

With tomatoes: put thickly sliced tomatoes over the buttered foil, add the fish and tie up as given above.

With mushrooms: put thinly sliced mushrooms over the buttered foil, add the fish and tie up.

With milk: smoked haddock may be poached in milk in a saucepan or a dish in the oven.

Do not wrap the fish, put into the pan with about $\frac{1}{4}$ pint milk, shake of pepper and $\frac{1}{2}-1$ oz. butter. Simmer gently on top of the cooker for about 10 minutes or allow 15–20 minutes in a moderately hot oven (400–425°F., Gas Mark 5–6). Smoked haddock, whether cooked in water or milk, can be topped with a poached egg. See also Kedgeree on page 77.

Halibut

This excellent fish has such a fine flavour that elaborate methods of cooking are not necessary.

Fried halibut

cooking appliance: boiling ring

Heat $1\frac{1}{2}$–2 oz. butter in the pan, add the well-dried, seasoned halibut steak and fry steadily for 4–5 minutes. Turn and cook on the second side for the same time.

Halibut does not need coating before frying.

To vary:

Halibut in brown butter: using $2\frac{1}{2}$ oz. butter, cook the fish as above then lift the fish on to a plate and allow the remaining butter to turn brown in colour by heating fairly quickly. Add a few drops of lemon juice or vinegar to flavour or a little chopped fresh parsley and/or a few capers. Pour the butter over the fish.

Halibut in tomato cucumber sauce: fry the halibut as above in the basic recipe but add 2 skinned, chopped tomatoes and a small piece of peeled, chopped cucumber to the pan, when cooking the fish on the second side. Pile the vegetable mixture on top of the fish.

Halibut in yoghourt: fry the halibut as in the basic recipe; tip a small carton of natural yoghourt into the pan when the fish is almost cooked, and heat gently. Serve this as a sauce on the fish, topped with paprika.

Parmesan halibut

cooking appliance: grill

Season the halibut well, brush with plenty of melted butter and grill for 4–5 minutes, turn and brush with more melted butter then grill for 3–4 minutes. Remove from under the grill and sprinkle the fish with grated Parmesan cheese. Return to the grill for 2 minutes.

Note:

Halibut is very good grilled, read the comments about grilling fish, page 33.

Roasted halibut

cooking appliance: oven

You can cook halibut in hot butter in an open oven-proof dish in the oven.

Heat 1–$1\frac{1}{2}$ oz. butter in an oven-proof dish, turn the seasoned fish in this until well coated with butter. Cook above the centre of a hot oven (425–450°F., Gas Mark 6–7) for approximately 15 minutes. Whole or halved tomatoes and mushrooms may be cooked round the fish.

Fresh herrings

These can be cooked by any of the basic methods, pages 32 to 34.

If the fishmonger has not removed the backbone do this yourself before cooking; particularly if you wish to put a stuffing in the fish. See if the fishmonger will do this for you or proceed as below.

To remove the backbone

1 Slit the stomach of the fish with a sharp knife and remove the roe and intestines. Throw these away but keep the roe.

2 Move the knife into the fish so you split it enough to open out.

3 Turn the fish with the cut side on to a plate or board and run your thumb against the centre backbone.

4 Turn the fish with the cut side uppermost and you will find you can lift the backbone out.

5 Wash and dry the herring and the roe and put the roe back in the fish, folding this back into its original shape, *or*

To fillet: cut flesh in 2 portions, i.e. fillets.

Note:

To avoid unpleasant smell of fish on your hands, wrap up the intestines and backbone in paper and put into the dustbin as soon as possible. Sprinkle about 1 teaspoon dry mustard on your hands and wash your hands in mustard and cold water before using soap.

Fried herrings

cooking appliance: boiling ring

Use very little fat as herrings contain a great deal of natural oil. The fish can be coated with well-seasoned flour or, if you have any rolled oats in the cupboard, dip the fish into a little milk then coat in seasoned rolled oats instead of flour.

Herrings left whole take approximately 10 minutes total cooking time. Do not over-cook otherwise the fish breaks. If cut into 2 fillets the cooking time will be 5 minutes only.

Fry the roe with the herring.

To vary:

Herring and lemon: fry the herring and roe and meanwhile halve a lemon, scoop out the pulp with a sharp knife and add this to the herring and fat in the pan. Heat for 1 minute.

With parsley, capers and tomatoes: fry the herring and roe and when nearly ready add a teaspoon chopped parsley, $\frac{1}{2}$ teaspoon capers and 2 chopped tomatoes. Heat for 2–3 minutes and pile the tomato mixture on to the herring.

Stuffed fried herrings

Use the fillings suggested for savoury grilled herrings.

Grilled herrings

Grill whole or filleted herrings as instructions on page 33.

They are particularly good served with a grilled bacon rasher or with halved tomatoes and/or mushrooms.

To vary:

Savoury grilled herrings: split the herrings and remove the backbone, as page 42.

Fill each herring cavity with:

a a little made mustard

b 1 or 2 chopped, pickled onions and a few capers

c 1 large, well-seasoned, sliced tomato.

Close the herring and grill as usual, turning very carefully so the filling will not fall out. Canned herrings *may be heated* for a few minutes under the grill.

Baked herrings

Herrings may be baked as the basic recipe on page 32, wrapping the fish in greased paper or foil or cooked on a covered oven-proof dish or plate. Herrings vary considerably in size, but a medium, whole, boned herring with the roe should take about 20–25 minutes.

The fish is much more interesting if stuffed before baking. The suggestions under grilled herrings could be used or try the following (each filling enough for 1 herring):

a **With fish paste:** sardine or anchovy fish paste; a salt flavour is excellent with herring. Use any paste left over as soon as possible.

b **With prawns or shrimps:** a few prawns or potted shrimps; these are excellent if mixed with the chopped roe and/or a chopped tomato.

c **With apple:** a small or half a large, peeled, diced dessert apple, blended with a few sultanas or chopped dates; allow an extra 5–8 minutes longer cooking.

d **With prunes:** a few stoned and well-drained, cooked or canned prunes; allow 5–8 minutes longer cooking.

e **With dates:** a few stoned, chopped dates, sprinkled with drops of lemon juice before using. This may sound strange but Arabic cooks use dates very successfully with fish and they blend well with herrings.

Canned herrings *may be heated topped* with the stuffing.

Pickled or soused herrings

I have not given recipes to prepare these in this

book as you are dealing with two very strong smelling ingredients – vinegar and fish, which would be very over-powering in your room. Instead I have given suggestions for using Rollmop and Bismarck herrings.

Herring salad

no cooking

you will need for 2 servings :

3 or 4 Bismarck or Rollmop herrings
1 desert apple

small piece of cucumber or a few gherkins
small carton natural yoghourt

to garnish :

1 or 2 tomatoes
½ lemon

1 small lettuce

1 Dice the herrings, the peeled and cored apple, peeled cucumber or gherkins.
2 Blend in a basin with the yoghourt.
3 Pile on a dish with quartered tomatoes, slices of lemon and quartered lettuce.
   To vary :
   With lemon or vinegar : use canned herrings and add a little lemon juice or vinegar to give a sharper flavour.
   With egg : add 1 or 2 chopped hard-boiled eggs and omit the apple.
   With beetroot : buy a tiny, cooked beetroot, peel, dice and add to the herring mixture just before serving.
   With corn : add the contents of a small can of corn (not creamed corn) and omit the apple.

Herring roes

First wash and dry the roes well on kitchen paper. The easiest and best ways to cook these are:

Poached in milk

cooking appliance : boiling ring

Put 6–8 oz. roes into a saucepan with ½ oz. butter, seasoning and 4 tablespoons milk. Simmer gently for 10 minutes. Serve on toast topped with paprika.

Fried herring roes

Wash and dry 8 oz. roes. Put 2 teaspoons flour on a plate or in a bag, add seasoning. Turn or shake the roes until coated then fry in 1–1½ oz. fat for 5 minutes. Serve with a salad or vegetables.

Steamed herring roes

cooking appliance : boiling ring

Put the roes with the ingredients above on one strong plate, cover with a second plate. Stand over a saucepan of boiling water and allow the water to boil steadily for 10 minutes. Serve on toast, topped with paprika.

Kippers

These are cooked as bloaters on page 35. One of the best ways to cook them is to 'jug' in boiling water for about 10 minutes, with a plate on top. You may be able to buy frozen kippers 'in a bag' and you simply cook according to the instructions given.

Lobster

Lobster salad

A lobster makes a delicious and luxurious salad for special occasions.
If using canned lobster meat, remove from the can and drain off the small amount of liquid you will find in the can. Flake the meat fairly coarsely and pile on to a bed of salad. Top with mayonnaise and garnish with sliced cucumber, tomato and sliced or quartered hard-boiled eggs.
If using fresh lobster you will need to prepare this first.
To prepare lobster : Ask the fishmonger to split this for you or split the fish lengthways with a sharp knife. Remove the dark vein from the flesh and also the grey 'fingers'. These should not be eaten. Either serve the two halves of the body and crack the large claws and remove the flesh from these or remove the flesh from the body and the claws and pile this neatly on to a bed of salad and serve with mayonnaise.

Lobster mornay

A very excellent way to serve lobster is to make a cheese sauce (see page 74), add the flaked lobster meat, then put this into a hot dish and top with a little grated cheese. If preferred, the lobster and cheese mixture may be put back into the halves of the fresh lobster.

Mackerel

These can be cooked like herrings, allowing just a little longer.

Plaice

This fish can be cooked in all basic methods, baked, fried, grilled, poached or steamed on pages 32 to 34.

It can also take the place of sole in the recipes given on pages 47 to 48.

Salmon

If you have a slice (cutlet) of fresh salmon, this is the best way to cook it. Season the fish lightly. Wrap the salmon in a piece of well buttered greaseproof paper NOT foil. Tie this, if possible, so the parcel stays quite neatly wrapped. Put the parcel into a saucepan of cold water (have enough water to cover the parcel of fish). Bring the water steadily to the boil.

If you intend to serve the fish hot

Allow the water to simmer gently for 5–6 minutes for a piece of fish weighing about 6 oz., lift the parcel on to a plate and open carefully.

If you intend to serve the fish cold

When the water has come to the boil, remove from the heat, put a lid over the saucepan or a plate if you have no lid. Allow the parcel of fish to stay in the water until this is quite cold. Lift out, open and serve.

To serve fresh salmon hot

The easiest accompaniment is just to top the salmon with chopped parsley and a knob of butter or just add the butter and serve with a generous wedge of lemon.

Mayonnaise is, however, a pleasant accompaniment to hot as well as cold salmon or you can turn this into tartare sauce as suggested under cold salmon.

To serve fresh salmon cold

Put the salmon on to a bed of lettuce and garnish with sliced tomato, sliced cucumber or gherkins and wedges of lemon. Serve with mayonnaise or tartare sauce.

Tartare sauce

no cooking

you will need for 2 servings :

3-4 tablespoons mayonnaise

1-2 gherkins, depending upon size

1-2 teaspoons chopped parsley

1-2 teaspoons capers

1 Put the mayonnaise into a basin, slice then chop the gherkins fairly finely and add.
2 Add the chopped parsley and capers. If you have no parsley use the larger amount of capers.

To serve canned salmon hot

Canned salmon may be made into a hot dish quite easily.

Spread a small amount of butter, approximately ½ oz. on to a strong plate. Add any flavouring wished, see below.

Open the can of salmon, put on to the plate, trying to keep the fish in as neat a shape as possible. Cover carefully with a soup plate or foil, so you do not break the portion of fish. Stand over a pan of boiling water and allow the water to simmer for 10 minutes.

Flavourings to add

Mushroom : slice about 2 oz. mushrooms and put on top of the butter, season lightly then add the salmon portion.

Tomato : slice 1 or 2 tomatoes and put on top of the butter, season lightly then add the salmon portion.

Asparagus : this is very easily over-heated; therefore, steam the salmon for 5 minutes, lift off the soup plate or foil, add the contents of a small can of asparagus which should be well drained.

To serve canned salmon cold

Either serve the portion of salmon on a bed of salad as given for fresh salmon or put the salmon into a basin, remove the skin if not desired, and the bones. Flake the salmon with a fork and add:

a chopped hard-boiled egg
b diced gherkins or cucumber
c a little mayonnaise and a few capers.
   Pile on to the bed of salad.

Salmon fish cakes

cooking time : 6 – 7 minutes
cooking appliance : boiling ring

you will need for 1 serving :

1 small can salmon (pink quality suitable)

3-4 oz. prepared dehydrated potato or 3-4 oz. mashed potato seasoning

to coat :

1 egg yolk or little milk   1 oz. crisp breadcrumbs

to fry :

½-1 oz. fat (use smaller amount for a silicone pan)

1 Drain the canned salmon – to do this, open the can only a little way and allow the liquid to pour away, this saves any possibility of the mixture being too moist.
2 Put the salmon into a basin, remove the skin and the bones, mash with a fork together with the potato, season well.
3 Take about one third of the mixture and form into a round flat cake, do the same with the remaining fish and potato, then coat as directed for fish, page 33. If, by chance, the mixture is very damp then coat in flour before the egg and crumbs, or if you do not want to use egg then just brush with milk.
4 Heat the fat in the pan and fry the cakes on either side until crisp and brown, drain on absorbent paper. These tend to be more moist than the frozen or ready-made variety so they need careful turning.

Note :

You can serve these as an hors d'oeuvre for 3 people with tomatoes.

To vary :

If you do not wish to fry the cakes then bake in the oven for approximately 15 minutes on a well-greased heated plate or tin.

Use cooked white fish or tuna instead of salmon.

Salmon hash

Prepare as for fish cakes but spread the fish and potato mixture over the frying pan when the fat is hot, cook for a few minutes until golden brown on the under side, then fold like an omelette and serve.

Salmon pie

cooking time : 25 – 30 minutes
cooking appliance : oven

you will need for 2 servings :

1 medium sized can salmon (pink quality suitable)

small can tomato soup* or small can tomatoes

small packet frozen peas or small can peas seasoning

to cover :

1 small packet dehydrated potato

½ oz. margarine or butter

* Ordinary consistency – not condensed.

1 Open the can of salmon, remove bones and skin if wished, but retain the liquid.
2 Put into an oven-proof dish with the whole of the can of soup or tomatoes if you like a moist texture. Or use ½ can of the soup if you like a firmer texture, or drain away the liquid from the canned tomatoes. This liquid could be saved for a day and added to a stew instead of water; the remaining soup can be stored.
3 Add the peas, if using frozen peas remember they will provide a little extra liquid, but drain the liquid from canned peas, season.
4 Spread the mashed potato (prepared according to the directions on the packet) over the fish, top with tiny pieces of margarine or butter.
5 Bake in the centre of a moderate to moderately hot oven (375–400°F., Gas Mark 4–5) until crisp and golden brown on top.

To vary :

With other fish : use other fish instead of salmon – tuna is particularly good, or cooked white fish or defrosted frozen or canned prawns.

With soup : use condensed soup and dilute with milk to give a creamy consistency. You then need only ½ can of condensed soup diluted with the same amount of milk for a moist texture; or ¼ can of soup diluted with the same amount of milk for a firmer textured filling.

With eggs : put 2 sliced hard-boiled eggs over the fish before adding the soup or tomatoes.

With mushrooms : add 2 oz. sliced mushrooms over the fish before adding the soup.

Scallops

The fish may be cooked whole or sliced and

with the white flesh and orange roe together. Remove from the shell. You may find a little moisture on the inside of the shell, keep this as it contains flavour; but generally the fishmonger cuts the fish off the shell and the liquid is lost.

Poached scallops

cooking time : 9 – 12 minutes
cooking appliance : boiling ring

you will need for 1 serving :

1 large or 2 smaller scallops	1 level teaspoon cornflour or
¼ pint milk	2 teaspoons flour
seasoning	½ oz. butter

to garnish :
small piece lemon

1 Either cook the fish whole or cut it into slices and simmer in most of the milk, season lightly. Cover the pan so the milk does not evaporate.
2 Blend the cornflour or flour with the rest of the milk and stir into the pan, adding the butter.
3 Cook steadily until thickened, taste and add more seasoning if wished.
Serve on the shell or in a dish with the lemon.
To vary :
Scallops au gratin : continue as above, and when cooked and in the shell, top with breadcrumbs and brown under the grill.
Scallops mornay : cook as above and when the fish is tender add 1 oz. grated Parmesan or 2 oz. grated Cheddar cheese to the sauce. Top with crumbs and grated cheese if wished and brown under the grill.

Fried scallops

cooking time : 6 – 7 minutes
cooking appliance : boiling ring

you will need for 1 serving :

1 large or 2 smaller scallops

to coat :

little milk or part of an egg	few crisp breadcrumbs

to fry :
½-1 oz. fat or
1 fat rasher bacon

to garnish :
small piece lemon

1 Dry the fish well, then coat in milk or egg and crumbs. Keep the scallop whole for this dish.
2 Heat the fat or fry the rasher of bacon and keep warm at one side of the pan while you fry the scallop. Serve with the bacon and lemon.

Scampi

Allow frozen scampi to defrost sufficiently so you may separate them.

To fry in butter

cooking time : 5 – 6 minutes
cooking appliance : boiling ring

you will need for 1 serving :

approximately 4 oz. uncooked frozen scampi	2 oz. butter
	few drops lemon juice or vinegar
seasoning	

to garnish :
lemon

1 Separate the scampi and dry on kitchen paper then season lightly.
2 Heat the butter and fry the scampi until tender, adding a little lemon juice or vinegar.
3 Garnish with sliced lemon.
Scampi may also be purchased ready coated in crumbs or you can buy them uncoated and coat them yourself as page 33, then fry them in hot butter or fat as in the recipe above. There is no need to add lemon juice in this case. Serve with tartare sauce, see page 45.

Sole

Sole is often called the aristocrat of white fish. You may find difficulty in buying one or two fillets of sole, so this may be the kind of dish you will prepare when you have more than one person at a meal. On the other hand, sole may be cooked as a whole fish. Follow the basic instructions for frying, grilling, baking, on pages 32 to 34. The only preparation you need to make with whole sole is to remove the head or ask the fishmonger to do this. The following recipes, however, are using fillets of sole and the fishmonger will fillet the sole for you.

Sole in tomato sauce

cooking time : 15 minutes
cooking appliance : boiling ring

you will need for 2 servings :

4 small fillets sole
seasoning
1 oz. butter
1 small onion or a little
  dehydrated onion

2 large tomatoes
4 tablespoons water,
  white wine or cider

1 Dry the fillets well and season.
2 Heat the butter. Fry the sole on either side for
1 minute. Lift out of the pan or push to one
side of the pan.
3 Fry the chopped or grated onion with the
skinned, chopped tomatoes in the butter for a
few minutes.
4 Add the liquid, a little extra seasoning, then
return the fish to this mixture and cook gently
until tender.
This is an adaptation of Sole Americane.

Sole with grapes

Fry the sole in hot butter as given in the recipe
above. When nearly tender lift out of the pan.
Add approximately 4 tablespoons white wine
and 4 tablespoons thin cream together with
about 8 halved de-seeded grapes. Heat for 2 or
3 minutes, put the sole back into this liquid and
finish cooking.
This is called Sole Veronique.

Lemon sole mornay

Fry or grill the lemon sole as the basic instructions on pages 33 and 34. Meanwhile make a
cheese sauce as the recipe on page 74. Put the
sole on to a hot serving dish and cover with the
sauce.
Note :
Small fillets of sole or plaice may be used
instead of the lemon sole.

Trout

This delicious fish can be obtained fresh or
frozen. If using frozen fish there is no need to
defrost this first.
Trout may be fried, grilled or baked as the
basic methods on pages 32 to 34
When you buy frozen trout you will generally
find you have to buy two trout, one is enough

for a medium portion.
If you have a refrigerator you can store the
extra trout in the freezing compartment according to the directions on the packet.

Trout and almonds

cooking time : 13 – 15 minutes
cooking appliance : boiling ring

you will need for 2 servings :

2 fresh or frozen trout
seasoning

1½ oz. butter
1 oz. flaked almonds

1 Remove the head and backbone from the trout,
season.
2 Heat the butter in the frying pan. Cook the fish
for approximately 10 minutes. Move to one
side of the pan.
3 Fry the almonds. Pour the nuts over the fish.
This is called Trout Grenoblaise.
To vary :
With breadcrumbs : if you have no nuts then fry
coarse breadcrumbs instead.
With lemon and capers : it is very pleasant if the
nuts are mixed with tiny pieces of lemon pulp
and a few capers.

Trout in cream sauce

Follow the recipe for trout and almonds. When
the fish and nuts are cooked, lift from
the pan on to a hot serving dish. Add 3 tablespoons thin or thick cream, heat for 1 minute
only, pour over the fish.

Trout in yoghourt

Fry the trout in the butter and add a small
carton of natural yoghourt and heat for 2 or 3
minutes. Omit the nuts but you may add
chopped parsley and/ or capers to taste if wished.

Trout meunière

Cook the trout as with almonds but omit the
nuts. When the trout is tender lift on to a hot
serving dish. Add a few drops of vinegar or
lemon juice to the butter and heat until this
turns a dark golden brown. Pour over the fish.
Note :
You may need to be a little more generous with
the butter.

Using smoked trout

Smoked trout is trout that has already been made sufficiently tender so it may be eaten without cooking. It can be cooked in any of the methods given, but you will halve the cooking time.

Tuna

This can be used in salads, etc. in place of salmon or in any hot dish where salmon is suggested.

If you have a small quantity of tuna left, stir into mayonnaise to serve over potato salad or see tuna sauce, to serve with veal, on page 55.

Turbot

Turbot is excellent in any recipes given for halibut.

Whiting

Whiting is excellent in any recipes given for sole.

Cooking with meat

Meat is another protein food and it is one of the foods that, with eggs, cheese and fish, should be served as a main dish.

Even with limited cooking appliances there are many ways in which you can prepare meat. I have avoided the usual roast joints as a joint generally is too large for one person. There may be occasions however, when you are entertaining friends and you could cook a joint and you will find instructions for this in most general cookery books. In this chapter I have concentrated on the quicker methods of preparing meat, i.e. frying, grilling, together with simple casseroled dishes. You will find the recipe for the basic 'pot roast' so that you can cook a fairly substantial piece of meat in a saucepan.

Choosing meat

As meat is a very expensive commodity, it is worth taking care in shopping for this. Many supermarkets have excellent meat counters but you will probably find the assistant has less time to give you help and advice than in a private butcher's shop.

Cuts of meat

In the following sections on different kinds of meat, you will find the cuts of meat that are available. Many of these will not be suitable for limited cooking facilities as they need prolonged simmering or roasting as a joint. *This will denote the joints that are less suitable for buying in small quantity.*

To choose beef:

Beef should have some fat, as this denotes a good quality and will give meat a moist texture as well as being tender. The fat should be a very pale cream in colour and look firm.

Cuts of beef

Aitchbone* (Between top rump and topside)	Roast if good quality, or boil or pickle.
Bladebone*	Stew or braise.
Brisket	Stew or braise, pickle or boil, or roast slowly.
Clod*	Stock for soups.
Fillet	Roast, grill or fry.
Flank*	Stew or braise, pickle or boil, or use for stock for soup.
'Leg of Mutton'* (Cut from shoulder)	Roast very slowly, stew or braise.
Marrowbone*	Use for stock for soup.
Oxtail*	Stew, braise or use for stock for soup.
Ribs*	Roast
Rump	Roast, grill or fry.
Shin* or leg	Stew, pickle or boil, use for stock.
Silverside	Pickle or boil.
Sirloin	Roast, grill or fry.
Skirt or chuck*	Stew or braise.
Topside	Roast or braise.
Neck*	Use for stock for soup.

In addition, when you shop for steak you may also be offered a wide choice.

Minute steak	Very thin slice of steak which needs cooking for 1 minute only on each side.
Rump steak	Full of flavour but not so tender as fillet.
Fillet steak	Lean, very tender.
Sirloin steak	Excellent proportion of lean and fat; cut from across the sirloin.
Entrecôte (Cut from middle ribs or sirloin)	Tender, good flavour. Generally a large piece that serves 2.
Point steak	Most tender. Cut from pointed end of rump.
Porterhouse*	Very large sirloin steak – up to 4 lb.
Planked steak*	Served on wooden plank, hence the name.
Tournedos	Fillet steak tied into a circle with string and served with variety of garnishes.

As you know both beef and veal come from the same animal and in this country it is often said that much of the veal that is sold is really young beef.

To choose veal

Veal is less popular in this country than on the Continent, so you may not be able to buy at all times. Veal spoils easily, so should be stored with great care. The fat of veal (of which there is very little) should be firm, white in colour and dry looking. The lean should be very pale pink and firm in texture.

Cuts of veal

Breast	Roast or boil.
Chops from loin	Grill or fry.
Chump end of loin	Roast.
Feet*	Boil, or use for stock for soup.
Fillet	Roast or fry, stew or braise.
Knuckle	Stew or braise.
Leg	Thin slices – grill or fry. Whole* – roast.
Loin*	Roast.
Neck	Best end – roast. Chops from best end – grill or fry. Middle* and scrag end* – stew or braise.
Head*	Boil or use for brawn.

To choose bacon

See that bacon looks moist and not hard and dry. If you like bacon with flavour, choose the traditionally cured bacon. If, on the other hand, you like a very mild bacon then you will prefer a sweet cure. Recipes for using bacon are on page 55.

Cuts of bacon

Forehock* (Sometimes divided into hock and knuckle)	Boil – a less tender but more economical joint than gammon so needs longer cooking.
Streaky (Often divided by specialists into top, prime, long)	Although can be used for a joint usually cut into rashers. Best buy *top or wide* streaky less fat – fry or grill.
Flank*	Boil.
Gammon (Divided into hock – or knuckle)	Boil.
Middle	Roast, grill, fry when cut into thick rashers. Often called steaks.
Corner	Boil.
Slipper	As middle.
Oyster cut*	Boil.
Back (Often divided into long and short back)	Cut in rashers and grill, fry or roast.
Collar	As forehock.

To choose lamb or mutton

Although lamb and mutton are given together in this section, it is important to allow longer cooking for mutton and to realise that unless it is of very good quality it is better to cook mutton by slower roasting and to avoid frying or grilling.

Lamb will have a certain amount of fat (although generally less than mutton), which should be firm but rather transparent-looking; the lean should be paler pink than mutton. Mutton, when of good quality, should have firm white fat and the lean meat should be deep pink.

Cuts of lamb and mutton

Breast of lamb or mutton	Roast or stew or braise or boil.
Chops from the loin	Mutton – if young, fry or grill; if older, use in casserole or cook steadily in the oven. Lamb – grill or fry.

Cutlets	See chops.
Head*	For soup or stock, or use in brawn.
Leg* (Divided in fillet of leg and shank end of leg)	Roast, stew, braise or boil.
Loin*	Roast.
Neck*	Best End – roast. Middle – stew, braise or boil. Scrag end – boil, soup or stock.
Saddle* (A double loin)	Roast.
Shoulder*	Roast, stew, braise or boil.
Trotters (Feet)	Soup or stock.

To choose pork

The fat of pork should be white and must be firm. DO NOT buy pork if the fat looks 'flabby' and soft. The lean of pork should be pale pink and firm.

Cuts of pork

Belly*	Boil.
Chops (From loin or spare rib)	Roast, fry or grill.
Head*	Boil or use in brawn.
Leg* (Generally called 'knuckle' of pork)	Roast or boil.
Loin*	Roast or boil.
Trotters*	Use for stews, brawn.

Pre-packed meat

Much of the meat sold in supermarkets today is pre-packed. When you get the meat home you can keep it in the wrapping if cooking within a few hours. If you buy this, however, and you are storing it in the larder or refrigerator for the next day, it is advisable to make a slit in the top wrapping to allow air circulation in the package.

Pre-packed bacon

Much of the bacon today is sold in polythene bags or wrapping. It is quite all right to keep bacon in these as the meat is cured and does not need the air circulation as fresh meat does. The packages often bear a date, check on this date before you buy the bacon.

To choose offal

Offal is the name given to special cuts of meat and the following information gives the most satisfactory methods of cooking offal.

Brains	Calf's, etc. can be served in a sauce or fried, etc.
Chitterlings (The small intestines of pig, sold ready prepared by pork butchers.)	Serve cold or fry in a little hot fat.
Feet or trotters	Pig's, calf's, lamb's are generally used to make meat moulds or brawn because they contain a great deal of gelatine.
Faggots	Generally sold ready-cooked by pork butcher. Made from liver, kidney, belly of pork, with crumbs, onion, etc.
Heart	Lamb's, calf's, pig's, ox. When tender, can be stuffed and roasted or braised.
Kidneys	Lamb's, calf's, pig's – fry or grill. Ox kidney – generally used in stewing.
Liver	Calf's, pig's, lamb's – fry or grill. Ox – braise.
Pig's Fry (The term given to a selection of offal from pig, including kidney and liver.)	Fry or bake in oven.
Sweetbreads (Lamb's or calf's – come from the pancreas, throat and heart of the animal)	Very easily digested. Fresh sweetbreads are often difficult to obtain, butchers now sell frozen sweetbreads. Use in a fricassée or braised in various sauces.
Tripe (From the stomach of the animal)	This is such a cheap and easily digested meat that it is worth cooking, see page 93. Ask for 'dressed' tripe which needs far less cooking time.

The kind of offal that you will not want to cook in a bedsitter, e.g. head, tail, etc., have been omitted.

Cooked meats

Many butchers' shops and most supermarkets have an excellent cooked meat counter and you will find a very wide selection of meats on sale. The following are the most usual but in addition you will find a wide selection of garlic sausage, salami, etc., offered.

Fortunately you may buy small quantities of cooked meat, so it is a good opportunity to try these.

Black pudding	A British sausage made with pig's blood, suet, breadcrumbs and oatmeal.
Brawn	A jellied British mixture of boned meat from pig's head.
Brisket	If pressed and glazed this is known as pressed beef. It is often salted.
Belgian salami	A smoked, dried and well-seasoned pork and beef salami.
Cabanos	A very well-spiced garlic sausage.
Castalet	A slightly milder sausage.
Cervelat	A mild, smoked pork sausage.
Chopped pork	A mild, inexpensive luncheon meat.
Coarse-cut liver sausage	This is generally more spicy than the British liver sausage.
Continental liver sausage	This is generally more spicy than the British liver sausage.
Corned beef	A canned preparation of cooked, pickled beef.
Danish salami	A rather salty pork sausage. Can be heated.
Extrawurst	An extra fine pork sausage, delicately seasoned.
Faggots	A country-type savoury dish with pork, pig's liver and kidney. Now commercially made and generally very good.
Frankfurters	Continental sausages to serve cold, or reheat.
French garlic sausage	A very highly seasoned sausage.
Garlic sausage	A high percentage of garlic, coarse-cut pork and ham. Serve cold.
German salami	Mainly pork, reasonably mild. There are a number of varieties – Mettwurst, Tyrol sausage, Teewurst, Kerkawer, Kraatwurst and Bleuwurst.
Haggis	Traditional Scottish dish made of liver, oatmeal and other ingredients. Cook steadily in water for approximately 1 hour. Serve hot.
Ham	Various grades of ham, both on bone and pressed.
Haslet	Not unlike faggots.
Hungarian salami	Very mild, yet slightly sharp, pork salami.
Italian salami	These vary, some being rather finely minced meat with pieces of fat, others of coarser texture. Generally mild in flavour.
Jellied veal	Veal set in a jelly like brawn.
Liver pâté	A paste of the foie gras type made from the liver of game, poultry or meat. Usually served as an hors d'oeuvre.
Liver sausage	A smooth textured and inexpensive sausage.
Luncheon meat	This contains a variety of mild pork and ham, mixed. Suitable for serving cold or reheating in slices.
Luncheon sausage	Similar to luncheon meat, but round in shape.
Ox tongue	Rolled and pressed. Bought sliced, in cans or glasses.
Parma ham	A very expensive, smoked ham which is generally served as an hors d'oeuvre with pieces of melon.
Polish salami	A dried, somewhat highly seasoned, sausage of pork.
Polony	An inexpensive sausage in red skin.
Pressed silverside	This is commercially pressed beef.
Saveloy	An inexpensive British, fairly highly seasoned, red-skinned sausage. Serve cold or reheat.
Strasbourg liver sausage	This is pork blended with the liver.
Tongue sausage	This is finely minced, in a sausage shape.
York ham	This is considered Britain's best type of cured ham.

Canned meat

Many meats are obtained in canned form but some of the most useful are:

Corned beef	A can holds 12 oz., so it may be wise to buy this by weight.
Ham	You will either find this sold as cooked ham or chopped ham and pork.
Luncheon meat	Various kinds, see page 61 for recipes.
Stewing steak	There are a variety of stewing steaks with vegetables, with various flavourings.
Tongue	You will probably find it better to buy the small cans of calf's tongue as many tins of ox tongue are large.

Basic recipes with meat

This section gives the most simple recipes for cooking the meats described in the previous pages.

Boiling meat

This is a method that I use very little in this book for most meat needs to boil or, to be more correct, simmer for a prolonged period and it seems to me that you would not wish the steam in your bedsitter and possibly you would not wish to deal with such a large piece of meat. However, you may want to cook a small piece of gammon by boiling and the method is given below. You could use this method for other pieces of meat in the lists on the preceding pages.

To boil gammon

I have chosen this piece of meat as this is so tender and the cooking time is not very long. Some of the joints of the 'sweet cured' bacon in polythene wrapping could be used.

Often the timing is given on the wrapping. To prevent gammon being over salt, put in a saucepan or large container of cold water and leave overnight or during the day. Throw this water away before you cook the gammon. Sweet cure bacon does not need soaking. Put the bacon into a large saucepan with enough water to cover, add a shake of pepper but no salt. Allow the water to come to the boil then lower the heat and cover the pan.

Timing: allow 40 minutes per lb. with the water gently simmering. A 1 lb. piece of gammon is enough for 2 or 3 good helpings. Naturally, if you buy a piece on the bone you must allow longer for cooking.

To give additional flavour: onions and carrots, etc. give rather a strong smell, so if serving the gammon as a hot dish I suggest you tip a can of (*a*) carrots, (*b*) broad, haricot or green beans, (*c*) a packet of mixed frozen vegetables into the saucepan and either heat the canned vegetables or cook the frozen vegetables until tender. Lift the meat on to a serving dish and then spoon the vegetables from the liquid and serve round the meat. The bacon stock is excellent for making a home-made soup.

Gammon or bacon is very delicious if cooked in:

a cider instead of water
b half ginger beer and half water
c half pineapple juice (canned) and half water.

Frying and grilling meat

Frying or grilling meat can produce a moist, delicious texture. Because these ways of cooking *are* so quick, the meat must be of high quality and this naturally means higher prices. Tough meat will never be made tender – it needs longer, slower cooking, stewing or casseroling. NEVER OVERCOOK when frying or grilling, otherwise meat becomes hard and dry. Cook the outside of the meat quickly so you seal in the meat juices and the flavour. Serve as soon as possible after cooking.

Frying meat

Meat is generally fried in shallow fat – enough butter, fat, oil to give good $\frac{1}{4}$ inch in pan, i.e. in a small pan you need about 1 tablespoon, about 1 oz. No fat is needed for bacon, fat pork or with 'non-stick' pans. Heat fat until very faint haze is seen or a cube of stale bread turns golden brown in 1 minute. Put meat, lightly seasoned (sometimes coated) into fat, cook quickly for about 2 minutes to seal outside and retain maximum flavour. Turn, using tongs, fish slice, knife but NOT a fork, which pierces meat and allows juice to flow. Fry on second side. Reduce heat so meat will cook through to centre without over-cooking outside. When cooked, lift meat from pan. Drain.

To drain fried foods, either hold for a few seconds over the pan to allow fat to drop back or drain on a double thickness of absorbent paper for ½ minute and serve.

Grilling meat

Heat grill for several minutes before cooking meat – except for bacon. Put meat, lightly seasoned, on grid of grill pan. To minimise washing up, line base of grill pan with aluminium foil. Brush a little oil, melted butter or fat with pastry brush over lean part of meat, to prevent hardening and drying. Cook rapidly for approximately 2 minutes to seal outside, turn with tongs. Season, brush second side of meat. Cook for the same length of time. With thick pieces of meat lower grill temperature, also move grill pan further away from heat if possible – cook more slowly until meat is ready. You need not drain grilled foods (one of the advantages over frying) for they are not 'fatty' and generally considered more easily digested than fried food.

Cuts to choose for frying and grilling

Beef steaks: fillet – most lean and tender. Rump. Sirloin. Entrecôte – not quite so tender, excellent flavour.

Cooking: 5–15 minutes depending on thickness and personal taste.

Minute: 1 minute either side.

Lamb or Mutton*: loin or gigot, best end neck chops or cutlets.

Cooking: 10–15 minutes.

*Steam mutton cutlets for 10 minutes before frying then coat.

Pork: loin. Chump or spare rib chops.

Cooking: 15–20 minutes. Snip fat to encourage this to crisp.

Veal: loin, best end neck chops, thin slices from leg called fillets (when cooked – escalopes).

Cooking: 15–20 minutes. Fillets generally coated.

Bacon: rashers of streaky, gammon, back (thick back rashers often called bacon chops), prime collar.

Cooking: few minutes only for thin rashers: cook both sides of thick rashers quickly, reduce heat to cook middle. To prevent fat curling, put into cold pan or heat grill as bacon is placed under. Remove rind or snip fat to encourage to crisp.

Accompaniments to fried meats

Fried tomatoes, mushrooms, onions: heat little fat in pan, fry vegetables steadily until tender. Tomatoes – should be halved, seasoned, adding a pinch of sugar. Mushrooms – peeled or washed well and stalks trimmed. Onions – peeled, sliced. For crisp onions, dip in milk or milk and flour (be careful though about the lingering smell in a living room).

Accompaniments to grilled meats

Grilled tomatoes and mushrooms: with grill pan with wide wire mesh grid, put in pan below with meat on top. Add seasoning and butter. Cook at same time as meat. With more solid grid, season, add little butter, heat under hot grill for few minutes. Put meat on grid, continue cooking. NOT suitable for onions.

To add a new flavour to fried steak

Curried steak: flavour the uncooked steak with a good shake of salt, cayenne pepper (very hot) and curry powder before frying.

Steak Diane: fry very small, chopped onion lightly before frying the steak. When the meat is cooked, flavour with a few drops of Worcestershire sauce and a little brandy if wished.

In cream and brandy: fry a chopped onion very lightly in the pan before adding the meat, cook meat and onion until nearly ready, then pour over ¼ pint thin cream and 1 tablespoon brandy. Heat gently and serve.

In sour cream: when the steak is nearly cooked lift on to a plate. Stir about ¼ pint dairy soured cream or single cream in the pan and the juice of ½ lemon. Heat for 2–3 minutes then add steak and finish cooking.

In paprika sauce: as in sour cream but blend 1 level teaspoon of paprika with the cream before adding to the pan.

Peppered steak: pepper the steak well on either side before frying. The classic method for 'steak au poivre' is to crush peppercorns and press them against each side of the steak before frying. Add cream and brandy if wished.

In tomato purée: fry several well seasoned tomatoes in the butter until soft then cook the steak in this.

In vegetable medley: use double the amount of butter and fry 2 oz. thinly sliced mushrooms, 3 sliced tomatoes and 1 chopped green pepper for 5 minutes. Add the steak and cook in the vegetable medley.

Mexicaine steaks: fry 2 chopped onions in the butter before adding the steaks. When the meat is nearly cooked add a small can of corn (not creamed) and a small can of sliced red peppers. Heat and season well.

Waldorf steaks: as Mexicaine steaks but use green instead of red pepper.

To add a new flavour to grilled steak

Sprinkle the steak with a few drops of Worcestershire sauce before cooking. Top with a thin layer of made mustard before cooking on the second side.

To add a new flavour to fried coated veal

One of the most popular dishes with veal is Weiner Schnitzel. In this, thin slices of veal (fillets) are coated with beaten egg, crumbs and fried. The veal is coated in the same way as fish, see page 33.

To vary:

a top with anchovy fillets and slices of lemon

b top with a fried egg

c top with tomato purée or tomato sauce, page 75, and a fried egg

d add a little curry powder to the crumbs used in coating the veal

e top with cream cheese just before serving the veal, allow $\frac{1}{2}$-1 oz. per person

f cook the veal, adding 2 oz. sliced mushrooms towards the end of the cooking period. Blend 1 teaspoon paprika with $\frac{1}{4}$ pint thin cream, pour over the meat and mushrooms and heat for 5 minutes.

To add a new flavour to fried uncoated veal

It is possible to fry veal without coating the meat, see page 53.

Flavourings are for 2 slices of veal or 2 veal chops.

Cook the meat and when nearly tender add:

soup: $\frac{1}{2}$ small can Mulligatawny soup and 1 tablespoon cream and heat.

wine or sherry: a wineglass of port wine or sherry and heat.

lemon and capers: fry the veal, lift out of the pan. Allow the butter to turn brown then add juice of $\frac{1}{2}$ lemon and 1 teaspoon of capers. Spoon over veal.

cream and sherry: when the veal is cooked add $\frac{1}{4}$ pint thin cream and 1 tablespoon sherry and heat for 2-3 minutes.

tuna and cream: when the veal is cooked lift out of the pan. Blend $\frac{1}{2}$ small can tuna with $\frac{1}{4}$ pint thin cream and heat for 3-4 minutes. Spoon over veal.

To add a new flavour to grilled veal

Cook the veal under the grill, as page 54. When nearly cooked top the meat with:

a **cheese**: a slice of Cheddar or Gruyère cheese, cook for 2-3 minutes until cheese melts.

b **cheese and ham**: a slice of cheese as above, cook for 1-2 minutes, remove from grill and top with a slice of cooked ham. Heat for 1 minute only.

c **bacon**: rasher of bacon; heat for 2-3 minutes.

d **yoghourt**: a little natural yoghourt; heat for 1-2 minutes.

e **mustard**: spread with French mustard and heat for 1 minute.

To add a new flavour to fried or grilled pork

Pork can be served with any of the flavourings suggested for veal. You can have thin slices of pork (fillets) cut from the leg of pork to take the place of veal.

To add a new flavour to fried bacon

With egg: dip the bacon rashers in beaten egg before cooking to give a firm crust.

With apple: fry rings of cored but not peeled apple with the bacon; pour a little cider over the apples and bacon before serving.

With canned fruit: fry rings of well-drained canned pineapple; stoned, canned or cooked prunes; halved canned peaches, with bacon. These are particularly good with gammon rashers.

To add a new flavour to grilled bacon

Grill thick rashers of bacon or gammon on one side, turn over and grill for a short time on the second side. When nearly cooked:

a spread a little made ordinary or French mustard over the bacon and cook for 2-3 minutes.

b blend mustard and sugar over the bacon and cook as **a**.

c add fruit as suggested in fried bacon.

To add a new flavour to fried lamb chops

In cream and cucumber: fry the chops and

when cooked lift out of the pan, pour away any surplus fat – the easiest way to dispose of fat is to pour it into a sheet of newspaper, roll it up and put into the dustbin, so it DOES NOT CLOG THE SINK.

Pour ¼ pint well-seasoned thin cream into the pan, with about 2 tablespoons chopped cucumber and plenty of seasoning. Heat for 1 minute then return the meat to the sauce and warm through.

With tomato purée: when the chops are nearly cooked add the contents of a small can of tomatoes and heat.

With savoury sauce: in addition to the tomatoes above, add chopped mushrooms or canned mushrooms, a shake of garlic salt.

Other variations

With pineapple: add rings of pineapple, which blend well with lamb, to the pan and heat through. You may also add chopped glacé cherries.

With soup: when the chops are nearly cooked, add ½ can vegetable soup to the pan and heat through.

With prunes: add a few canned or cooked prunes to the pan and heat, spoon a little prune juice over the meat.

To add a new flavour to grilled lamb chops

With orange: cut a large orange into thick rings and put under the grill for the last few minutes before the chop is cooked. Turn the rings so they absorb some of the juice from the chops.

With spaghetti and mushrooms: put a medium sized can of spaghetti into the grill pan and top with a layer of sliced mushrooms. This becomes heated as the chops cook and the fat from the meat 'bastes' the spaghetti.

Dealing with the fat after frying and grilling meat

Excess fat can be a nuisance in a small kitchen SO DO NOT POUR IT DOWN THE SINK, see under chops.

Wipe out the frying pan or grill pan with kitchen paper before washing up.

To choose chicken for frying and grilling

Fortunately, today the rearing of small plump chickens suitable for frying or grilling is a thriving industry and you will be able to buy joints of chicken from most good butchers or supermarkets. If the chicken is frozen do not try to cook it in this state, except in an emergency, for you will find the flavour is infinitely better if the chicken has thawed out. Dry the chicken well. If you wish you may coat it with egg and crumbs, see page 33.

To fry chicken

you will need to fry 1 joint:

At least 1 oz. of fat or a very good tablespoon of oil. Chicken is a lean meat that must be kept moist during cooking. Fry the chicken quickly on either side to brown, lower heat and continue cooking until tender, approximately 12–15 minutes.

To add a new flavour to fried chicken

With vegetables: fry sliced mushrooms and sliced tomato in a little extra fat. Lift out of the pan, cook chicken then return the vegetables to the pan for the last few minutes.

With creamed corn: fry the chicken until nearly tender. Push to one side of the pan. Add either a small can of creamed corn or corn kernels plus 2 tablespoons cream from the top of the milk. Heat and serve.

With banana: when the chicken is nearly cooked, fry a halved banana in the pan. If you serve this with corn and watercress you have a simple form of Chicken Maryland.

With walnuts: the Italians often serve walnuts with chicken. When the chicken is nearly cooked, add 1 oz. of halved walnuts with 2 tablespoons of cider or white wine and heat together.

Chicken chop suey: this is a very simple form of a Chinese type of dish.

Cut the chicken joint into small pieces, fry in the hot butter until nearly tender, adding a few chopped mushrooms towards the end of the cooking time. Add the contents of a can of bean shoots, a few pieces of sliced gherkin and heat together.

To grill chicken

If you would rather grill instead of fry chicken, this is a very pleasant way of cooking it. The quality of the chicken must be exactly as when frying.

Heat the grill, brush the chicken with plenty of melted butter or with oil and cook quickly on one side, turn, brush with more butter or oil and cook on the second side. Lower the heat and continue cooking until tender, approximately 12–15 minutes total cooking time.

To add a new flavour to grilled chicken

a Pour one or two tablespoons red wine over the chicken, allow to stand for an hour then grill as above.

b Spread a little French mustard over the chicken just before it is cooked.

c Blend the grated rind of a lemon or orange with the butter before cooking.

Casseroled dishes and stews

These are simple dishes to prepare in many ways, for you simply add the savoury ingredients to the meat and simmer gently. I am giving one or two rather special casseroles as an example and you can then develop your own choice of flavourings. I have given quantities for 2 servings since, IF YOU CAN STORE SAFELY, a stew may be reheated without spoiling the flavour. Always reheat thoroughly. I have avoided the traditional browning of the meat in fat; coating meat, etc., as I feel you can find these recipes are in most books and the following recipes are easier for you to try. I have used rather better quality meat than usual in a stew to shorten your cooking time. If, however, you do decide to use proper stewing meat, see tables listing meats, then *you will need to double the cooking time.*

Stew Americaine

cooking time : 30 minutes
cooking appliance : boiling ring

you will need for 2 servings :

8-12 oz. topside of beef, fillet of veal, 2 lamb chops or 2 joints frying chicken	1 can sweet corn kernels seasoning
1 medium can tomatoes	
2 oz. mushrooms	

1 Cut the meat into neat pieces about 1 inch square, unless using chops or joints of chicken.

2 Put into the saucepan with the tomatoes and simmer for 15 minutes.

3 Add the sliced mushrooms, corn and seasoning

and continue cooking until the meat is tender.

To vary :

With mixed vegetables : use canned or frozen mixed vegetables in place of corn and mushrooms.

With corned beef : use diced corned beef, in which case, heat the tomatoes, mushrooms and corn, then add the corned beef and heat through.

With kidneys : add part of a can of kidneys.

Curried meat or chicken No. 1

Use either this quick curry or you will find the proper curry sauce following.

cooking time : 10 – 15 minutes
cooking appliance : boiling ring

you will need for 2 servings :

8-10 oz. rump or other frying steak, fillet of pork, veal or lamb or 2 joints frying chicken	½ tablespoon chutney or marmalade* seasoning pinch sugar ½ tablespoon dried fruit – dates, sultanas
1 can Mulligatawny soup	
1 teaspoon curry powder	

to serve :

boiled rice, see page 76

*to give sweet taste

1 Cut the meat into neat pieces. The joints of chicken may be halved to make sure they are covered with the sauce.

2 Blend the soup and curry powder, put into the saucepan with the meat or chicken.

3 Add the rest of the ingredients and cook until the meat or chicken is tender. The time given assumes the meat to be of very good quality.

4 Cook the rice, put on to a hot dish or plates, serve the curry over this.

For accompaniments see below recipe No. 2.

To vary :

If using cooked meat, canned beef or luncheon meat, use rather less than the whole can of soup and simmer for 5–6 minutes only.

Instead of all Mulligatawny soup use about ¾ can and add 1 tablespoon tomato ketchup, few drops Worcestershire sauce, 1–2 teaspoons made mustard and a shake of garlic salt.

Curried meat or chicken No. 2

cooking time : 20 – 25 minutes
cooking appliance : boiling ring

you will need for 2 servings :

1 onion or leek	½ pint water
1 small apple	8-10 oz. meat as recipe
1 oz. margarine or	No: 1 or 2 joints
butter	frying chicken
1-2 teaspoons curry	chutney as recipe No. 1
powder	dried fruit as recipe No: 1
2 level teaspoons	seasoning
cornflour	

to serve :

boiled rice, see page 76

1 Peel and slice the onion or leek and apple, then fry in the hot margarine or butter for 3–4 minutes. Stir in the curry powder and cornflour, blended with the water.
2 Bring the sauce to the boil, stirring well to keep the sauce smooth. Add the rest of the ingredients and simmer gently in a covered pan until the meat is tender.
3 Cook the rice and serve as recipe No. 1.

Accompaniments to curries

Chutney, sliced banana, salted peanuts, grated raw carrot, cocktail onions, gherkins.

To vary :

This curry sauce is a basic one you can use in other ways, e.g.

If you wish to buy cheaper stewing meat, as in the tables on pages 49 to 51, then cut this into small pieces. Follow the method above, but increase the amount of liquid to ¾ pint to allow for the extra cooking period. Diced stewing beef will take about 1½ hours gentle simmering. If you wish to curry cooked meat by this recipe, dice the cooked meat (e.g. corned beef, ham). Make the sauce as stages 1–2, add the meat and heat : do not over-cook the meat in the sauce.

Curried fish : make the sauce as stages 1–2, add neat pieces of raw fish, e.g. cod, and simmer until tender. Prawns or other shellfish are excellent if used.

Curried eggs : make the sauce as stages 1–2, add 4 shelled hard-boiled eggs and heat.

Burgundy stew

This method of cooking meat, particularly for beef and veal, is excellent, for the wine tenderises the meat and gives a delicious colour to the sauce.

cooking time : 15 minutes
cooking appliance : boiling ring

you will need for 2 servings :

1 oz. small cocktail	seasoning
onions	½ pint red wine (any
2 oz. small button	Burgundy excellent)
mushrooms	pinch mixed dried herbs
8-10 oz. fillet of beef,	
2 joints of chicken	
or piece of gammon	
about 10 oz.	

to serve :

new or creamed potatoes

1 Put the onions, mushrooms and the diced meat or the chicken into a saucepan and season lightly then add the wine and herbs.
2 Simmer gently for approximately 15 minutes until the meat is tender.

To vary :

a To thicken the liquid:
Add a tablespoon dehydrated potato powder and stir very well.
Blend 2 level teaspoons cornflour with 2–3 tablespoons water, add to the stew when it is cooked, stir very well as the sauce thickens *or* if you have no cornflour use 1 level tablespoon flour but DO STIR VERY WELL WHEN ADDED, AS FLOUR IS MUCH MORE INCLINED TO BECOME LUMPY.
One of the easiest ways to thicken any stew is with bread. For the quantity above cut a slice from a small loaf of bread, it should be about ¼ inch thick. Remove the crusts, put the slice into the saucepan and allow it to simmer for about 5 minutes, then beat hard until it completely disintegrates. The bread should be added 5 minutes before the meat is cooked and the heat should be low when you do this.
b Use white instead of red wine, particularly suitable for chicken.
c Use cider instead of red wine, excellent with gammon.
d If using gammon, omit the mushrooms and add a peeled, cored, sliced apple (dessert variety) half-way through the cooking.

To make casserole dishes

Any of the stews given above could be cooked

in a well-covered casserole in a very moderate oven (300–325°F, Gas Mark 2–3). The time taken will be about 45 minutes instead of 15 minutes, and you could omit 1–2 tablespoons liquid, since you do not have the same evaporation in the oven.

Pot roast

A pot roast is an admirable way of preparing a meal in a saucepan, so the meat tastes like a roasted joint.

you will need for 4 servings :

2 oz. fat or margarine approximately	4 medium sized potatoes
2 lb. good quality meat	4 medium sized carrots
or	seasoning
2¼-2½ lb. roasting chicken	

1 Put 1 to 2 oz. fat or margarine into the largest, strongest saucepan you possess and heat.
2 Brown one side of the joint of meat or chicken, then turn and brown the second side.
3 Lift the meat out of the pan on to a plate. Pour away any fat, see page 56.
4 Put in the prepared vegetables (left whole), season lightly. Add just enough water to cover the vegetables; place the browned meat on top.
5 Cover the saucepan tightly with a lid; lower the heat and allow to cook very gently.
   Beef – for 2 lb. joint allow 1 hour
   Lamb, pork or veal – for 2 lb. joint allow 1 hour 15 minutes*
   Chicken – for a 2¼–2½ lb. chicken (weight when trussed) allow 1 hour

*if on the bone, but if solid meat allow 1 hour 30 minutes.

To serve : lift meat and vegetables out of saucepan on to a warm dish.
To make the gravy : blend 1½ teaspoons cornflour or 3 teaspoons flour, 1 teaspoon gravy browning with two tablespoons water.
Add the cornflour mixture to the liquid left in the pan (there should be about ½ pint liquid). Boil steadily until thickened, stirring all the time.

To give additional flavour :

a use ½ wine and ½ water in the pan.
b stuff the chicken – you can buy packet stuffings.
c add other vegetables during cooking, mushrooms, tomatoes, etc.

Sausages

Sausages may be fried, grilled or baked. Buy fresh sausages and allow 8 oz. for two people. You are given the choice of pork or beef, large or the small chipolata sausages. Unless told to the contrary, prick the skins lightly.
To fry : heat about ½ oz. fat in the pan and cook steadily for 10–13 minutes.
To grill : cook steadily for the same length of time; there is no need to add fat.
To bake : allow 20–25 minutes in a hot oven.

Toad in the Hole

Follow the directions for Savoury Puff on page 61; use 2 large or 4 small sausages in place of luncheon meat. Cook the sausages for 10–15 minutes before adding the batter.
Note :
You can heat cooked or canned sausages in light ale for a German touch.
Remember cooked sausages can be added to : stewed canned kidneys, omelettes (slice and add to eggs before cooking), and to salads.

Frankfurters

Frankfurters can be heated the same way as sausages and serve with a mustard tomato sauce.
Mustard tomato sauce : blend 1 teaspoon French mustard to each tablespoon tomato ketchup you use.

Frozen Hamburgers

Hamburgers and other frozen meat cakes (e.g. rissoles) are economical, interesting and convenient forms of meat. Remember that, like all types of meat, they are highly perishable when no longer frozen. Use as quickly as possible after purchase, unless storing in the freezing compartment of the refrigerator.
Follow the directions given on the packet for methods of cooking. You can also:

a **Use cheese :** add extra protein and flavour if you top the cooked Hamburgers with cheese and melt under the grill or sandwich two uncooked Hamburgers with the cheese and bake in the oven.
b **Use pineapple :** fry or bake the Hamburgers, basting them with pineapple syrup and serving with rings of pineapple.

c Use with curry sauce: use the Hamburgers instead of meat and cook in the curry sauce, page 58.

Canned stewing steak

This can be the basis for a quickly prepared dish. One small to medium sized can gives enough for 1 serving, but when baked beans, etc. are added, it will make 2 servings. The meat and liquid may just be heated or extra flavourings added.

Goulash

cooking appliance: boiling ring

Open a small can of tomatoes, blend with 1–2 teaspoons paprika in the saucepan and heat with a can of stewed steak. Serve with heated canned potatoes or canned or cooked spaghetti.

Curried stewing steak

cooking appliance: boiling ring

Blend 1–2 teaspoons curry powder and 2 teaspoons chutney or sweet pickle with the steak and heat. Serve with some of the accompaniments on page 58.

Hasty Cassoulet

cooking appliance: boiling ring

The quickest and most simple version of this classic dish is to heat a small can of baked beans, 1 sliced tomato, shake garlic salt and the canned stewing steak together. This would then make enough for 2 servings.

Rather more elaborate versions of the above recipe can be made by adding 1–2 oz. sliced garlic sausage or slice a Frankfurter sausage when the steak, etc. is hot, add this with a few cocktail onions and heat. Cooked lamb or poultry can be used instead of stewing steak with a small can of tomatoes to provide liquid.

Quick Moussaka

cooking appliances: oven and boiling ring

Slice 1 aubergine, sprinkle with salt and stand for 10 minutes. Peel and slice 2 potatoes. Fry the aubergine in 1 oz. fat. Put into a casserole with 1 potato, a can of stewing steak. Top with second sliced potato and ½ oz. butter. Cook for 1 hour in the centre of a very moderate to moderate oven (350–375°F., Gas Mark 3–4).

Canned or fresh kidneys

Using canned kidneys

The small cans of kidney are an excellent purchase, although somewhat expensive. You can heat them and serve:
a with grilled bacon and tomatoes
b on buttered toast
c as a filling for several omelettes or over hard-boiled eggs as a sauce
d add part of a can to the stew on page 57.

Fresh kidneys

Buy lamb's kidneys. Allow 1–2 per person. Remove the skin and halve the kidneys, take out any gristle. You can then:
a fry the kidneys with bacon in a little butter – they take 5–6 minutes.
b first fry, season, cover with a little port wine and simmer for 10 minutes.

Canned or cooked ham

Canned ham can be used in the recipes on the following pages, it can also produce other interesting dishes or served cold with salad.

Barbecued ham

Slice the ham. Sprinkle each slice with a little brown sugar. Fry in hot fat with rings of apple. Top with chutney before serving – when buying cooked ham buy 1 *thick* slice.

Pineapple roast

Open a small can of ham or buy about 8–12 oz. ham in one piece, put into a roasting dish. Mix 2 teaspoons sugar, 1 teaspoon mustard powder with 2 tablespoons pineapple syrup (from a small can pineapple). Put the drained pineapple cubes or rings round the ham and cook for 20–25 minutes in a hot oven.

Canned or cooked tongue

Although this is an excellent meat to serve

cold, it can be turned into an appetising hot dish.

Tongue Portuguese

cooking time: 10 minutes
cooking appliance: boiling ring

you will need for 2 servings:

6-8 oz. cooked or canned tongue	1 rasher bacon
1 oz. butter	wineglass port wine
few cocktail onions	shake pepper

to serve:

mixed frozen vegetables or toast

1 Cut the tongue into neat fingers and heat in the butter with the onions and diced bacon.
2 Add the liquid and pepper and heat.
Serve at once with the vegetables or toast.
To vary:
Heat tongue in tomato sauce, page 75.
Use stock and little orange juice instead of port wine.

Tongue in cherry sauce

Use small can of 6–8 oz. tongue. Cut the tongue in fingers.
Blend the juice from a small can of cherries and 1 level teaspoon cornflour. Heat until thickened. Put in the tongue, cherries and seasoning and heat.

Ways to turn canned luncheon meat into a meal

Buy the smallest sized can possible or you may be able to buy the meat by weight in a supermarket. Allow approximately 4 oz. per person, so a 7 oz. can will be enough for 2 servings. Corned beef may be used in similar ways.

Savoury puff

cooking time: 25 minutes
cooking appliance: oven

you will need for 1 serving:

1 tomato	1 egg
3-4 oz. luncheon meat	pinch salt
½ oz. fat	2 oz. flour
	¼ pint milk

1 Slice the tomato and heat, together with the diced luncheon meat, for 5 minutes in the hot fat. Put the dish towards the top of a hot oven (425–450°F., Gas Mark 6–7).
2 Meanwhile blend the egg with the other ingredients to make a smooth batter, pour over the meat and tomato. Return to the oven, keeping this fairly near the top.
3 Bake for approximately 20 minutes, then serve at once.

Luncheon meat grilled with cheese

cooking time: 5 – 6 minutes
cooking appliance: grill

you will need for 1 serving:

3-4 oz. luncheon meat	2 oz. Cheddar cheese
½ oz. butter	

to garnish:

1-2 tomatoes

1 Cut the meat into 2 slices, spread one side of each slice with the butter and cook for 2–3 minutes under a hot grill.
2 Turn and cover with thinly sliced or grated cheese and return to the grill with the halved tomatoes and continue cooking until the cheese melts.

Barbecued luncheon meat

cooking time: 15 minutes
cooking appliance: boiling ring

you will need for 2 servings:

7 oz. luncheon meat

for the sauce:

1 onion	½-1 tablespoon chutney
1 dessert apple	few drops Worcestershire
small can concentrated tomato soup	sauce

1 Dice the meat, slice the peeled onion.
2 Peel, core and dice the apple.
3 Put the soup with the onion and apple into a saucepan and simmer very gently for 10 minutes or until the onion is *just* soft.
4 Add the rest of the ingredients and simmer for 5 minutes.
See also risotto, page 77.

Liver

Liver is a very important food, like all meat

it provides protein to the body; it is also a rich source of iron.

For quicker cooking methods choose calf's or lamb's liver.

To fry liver

This can be fried as meat on page 53. The liver should be cut into $\frac{1}{4}$ inch slices; the butcher will do this for you. Allow 4–6 oz. per person. Season the liver and shake a light dusting of flour or cornflour over the meat then fry in hot butter or bacon fat, allowing approximately 6–7 minutes. A rasher of bacon can be added to the pan. Do not over-cook liver as it makes it tough.

To flavour liver

Orange liver: squeeze the juice of $\frac{1}{2}$ orange over the liver as it cooks.

Pour a little red wine over the liver as it cooks.

Liver in a stew

Diced calf's or lamb's liver may be used in place of steak in the stews.

Note:

Grilled liver – This is not very satisfactory as it dries badly in cooking.

Sweetbreads

If you can obtain sweetbreads, they are an excellent purchase, as they are not difficult to cook and are very easy to digest.

If you buy frozen sweetbreads, do not defrost before cooking as the "blanching" process does this. You also need to buy more frozen sweetbreads than fresh as they seem to lose weight as they thaw out.

Whether fresh or frozen the SWEETBREADS MUST FIRST BE BLANCHED. To do this put into cold water, bring to the boil and then throw away the water.

Fried sweetbreads

cooking time: 30 minutes
cooking appliance: boiling ring

you will need for 2 servings:

8 oz. fresh or 12 oz. frozen sweetbreads	seasoning

to coat:

1 egg yolk	2 tablespoons crisp breadcrumbs (raspings)

to fry:
1-1$\frac{1}{2}$ oz. fat

to serve:

lemon	watercress

1 Blanch the sweetbreads. Drain, then put into cold water with a little seasoning, bring the water to boiling point; lower the heat and simmer gently for 20 minutes.

2 Cool, then coat in the egg yolk and crumbs, as page 33. Remove any pieces of tough skin.

3 Fry in the hot fat until crisp and brown; this takes approximately 5 minutes.

4 Drain on absorbent paper. Serve with lemon and watercress.

See also fricassée of chicken and subsitute sweetbreads in place of the chicken, page 92.

Cooking meat in foil

Aluminium foil is an excellent wrapping for meat. You can line the grid of the grill pan with foil which enables you to catch the meat juices as the meat cooks, and saves some washing-up, see page 54.

In addition, you can wrap meat or meat and vegetables in a foil 'parcel' so eliminating the use of frying, grilling or baking pans.

Foil cooked steak

cooking time: 25 – 35 minutes
cooking appliance: oven

you will need for 1 serving:

$\frac{1}{2}$ oz. butter	seasoning
few mushrooms	portion fillet or rump
2 tomatoes	steak about $\frac{1}{2}$ inch thick

1 Cut a square of foil, large enough to wrap around the meat, spread with the butter.

2 Put half the sliced mushrooms and tomatoes on the foil, season lightly.

3 Place the steak on top and cover with the rest of the vegetables. Seal the foil firmly round the meat and vegetables.

4 It is a good idea to put the 'parcel' on a tin (a roasting tin is ideal) but if carefully wrapped no juice will come out.

5 Bake towards the top of a hot oven (425–450°F., Gas Mark 6–7), allowing about 25

minutes for under-done steak, up to 35 minutes for very well done steak. Open the parcel carefully.

To vary:

Without vegetables: omit vegetables, just cook the meat, in which case allow 4–5 minutes less cooking time.

With chops: lean lamb chops and veal and joints of chicken could be cooked in the same way.

Allow about 30 minutes. Pork chops are too fat.

With other meat: slices of veal, liver, halved kidneys, may also be cooked like this; allow 25 minutes.

With red wine: add a little red wine to the meat before sealing the foil.

Reheating meat

Reheating some of the meat dishes you buy.

Steak and other pies should be heated in the oven, but if you have no oven then put the pie on a plate over a pan of water, allow the water to boil quickly. DO NOT COVER THE PLATE. This allows the pastry to remain as crisp as possible.

Reheating slices of cooked meat or poultry

Many stores selling cooked meats have cold joints of meat for slicing. Obviously these are excellent for cold meals without any further attention, but the sliced meat can be heated easily. Choose rather under-done beef, allow 4 oz. for a generous portion. Either put the meat on a strong plate, cover with a second plate and cook for a few minutes over a pan of boiling water *or* make a small quantity of gravy or stock with water and part of a stock cube. Put the meat for a short time into the hot liquid. Serve with vegetables.

Cooking with vegetables

There are always plenty of vegetables you can buy today – fresh, frozen, canned and A.F.D. (Accelerated Freeze Dried – which means they are easy to store and need no soaking).

Plan plenty of variation in your vegetable dishes, for these provide you with roughage, vitamins and mineral salts and so contribute to a healthy diet.

Choosing vegetables

Fresh vegetables are easy to select and hints are given under each vegetable together with method of buying, i.e. by weight or singly.

Cooking vegetables

Although hints are given under each vegetable the important factors in cooking vegetables are given below.

1 The vegetables must be as fresh and clean as possible.

2 They should be put into boiling, salted water – use the minimum amount of water (approximately ½ inch only) for green vegetables. Boil rapidly, with the lid ON the saucepan, for the shortest possible time until just cooked.

3 Strain through a sieve or colander.

4 Serve topped with a little butter or margarine as soon as possible after cooking.

It must be remembered, however, that fresh vegetables have a very strong smell as they cook, green vegetables in particular. So if you have cooked these, wash the pan as soon as possible and throw away the water IMMEDIATELY unless you like to use it in a gravy or sauce. The water contains valuable vitamins and mineral salts *but* does have a penetrating and lingering smell. This is why in many cases it is suggested that raw, canned or frozen vegetables are probably easier to serve.

Raw vegetables retain even more vitamins than fresh, correctly cooked vegetables. The heat applied to vegetables when canning, does destroy some vitamins but frozen and A.F.D. vegetables are high in vitamin content.

Artichoke

There are two kinds of artichokes – the first a root, the second a green artichoke.

Jerusalem artichokes

Buy by weight, 8 oz. is enough for 2 portions as they are very substantial. You will not need potatoes when you serve these. They store well for several days before cooking.

When fresh: they are firm in appearance.

To prepare: first wash to remove soil. Scrape away the skin or peel thinly: this is quite difficult as the vegetable is an uneven shape. Put into cold water with a slice of lemon or teaspoon of vinegar, while preparing.

To cook: put into boiling salted water and simmer steadily for approximately 20 minutes.

To serve: with a little butter or margarine.

New way to serve: cold in a salad.

Jerusalem artichokes are not available other than fresh.

Globe artichokes

Buy singly. One is enough for a portion.

When fresh: green and firm with no brown marks on the leaves; you can store for 1 or 2 days only before cooking.

To prepare: see page 15.

To cook: see page 15.

New ways to serve: cold with prawn or other salad.

Other ways to buy Globe artichokes

In cans only. Sold as artichoke bottoms and are sometimes difficult to buy.

Asparagus

Asparagus is bought either in bundles or by weight. 4–6 oz. is enough for a person (as a small helping of vegetables), so a bundle may be too much, unless you intend to use part of the bundle and store the rest, or cook all the bundle and serve some hot and some cold. You can store for 1 or 2 days only before cooking.

When fresh: firm and green.

To prepare: see page 14.

To cook: see page 14.

New ways to serve: as a main dish coated with cheese sauce, added to meat, fish, poultry dishes.

Other ways to buy asparagus

In cans – you have the choice of thick white or green asparagus or just the tips. Very plentiful but they vary a lot in price. Frozen – you have very good quality, but they are sometimes difficult to buy.

Aubergine

Aubergines (egg plant) are bought singly al-though price is generally given by weight. One small aubergine is enough for 1 portion or 2 small portions.

When fresh: purple-black in colour, firm and unmarked, you can store for 2–3 days before cooking.

To prepare: wash well, either slice or halve.

New ways to serve: see below.

Aubergines are only available fresh.

Fried aubergine

cooking time : 8 – 9 minutes
cooking appliance : boiling ring

you will need for 2 servings :

1 small aubergine	seasoning
2 teaspoons flour	
	to fry :
	1 oz. fat

1 Wash and dry the aubergine, then cut into ¼ inch slices.
2 Mix the flour and seasoning on a plate and press the slices of aubergine against this. Aubergine skin has a somewhat bitter taste, so if you dislike this you can either peel the skin away before slicing or allow the slices to stand for 10–15 minutes before cooking.
3 Heat the fat and fry the slices on both sides.
4 Drain on absorbent paper and serve.

Stuffed aubergine

cooking time : 30 minutes
cooking appliances : boiling ring and
oven

you will need for 2 servings :

1 medium to large
   aubergine
little salt

for the filling :

small can stewed steak	1½ oz. butter
	½ oz. Parmesan
	cheese

1 Wash and dry the aubergine: to counteract the bitter flavour sprinkle the skin with salt and leave for 20 minutes before cooking.
2 Halve lengthways and simmer in boiling, salted water for 15 minutes, drain.

3 Cut out the centre pulp, chop this finely, leaving the outer case unbroken.

4 Meanwhile open the can of stewed steak, heat for 2–3 minutes in the saucepan until the rather solid mass of meat and gravy separate.

5 Spoon out the meat, leave the gravy in the saucepan and serve with the dish.

6 Mix meat and aubergine pulp.

7 Pile into aubergine cases and stand in a buttered dish.

8 Top with grated cheese and remainder of the butter and bake for 15 minutes towards the top of a hot oven (425–450°F., Gas Mark 6–7).

Beans

There are various kinds of beans you can buy, so they are listed separately. Green beans, i.e. runner beans, French beans, sold by weight. They weigh surprisingly light, 4 oz. is enough for 1 portion, particularly French beans (which are often sold by the 4 oz. weight).

Green beans

When fresh: firm and green, but not tough looking. You can store for 1 day before cooking.

To prepare: runner beans, cut off sides, top and bottom and cut into neat pieces.

French beans, prepare as above, leave whole.

To cook: in boiling salted water for 15 minutes.

To serve: with a little butter or margarine.

New ways to serve: cooked and cold in a salad or hot topped with grated cheese.

Other ways to buy green beans

Canned green beans are very easily obtained, just heat and serve as fresh beans.

Frozen green beans are also very easily obtained, cook as instructions and serve as fresh beans, you will find these described as 'sliced green beans', and Haricot Verts which are thin beans.

Accelerated freeze dried beans have become easily obtainable. Cook as instructions and serve as fresh beans. A very good purchase as you can use part of the packet.

Broad beans

These are sold by weight, often the pods are fairly empty so you need at least 8 oz. for 1 portion.

They store for 1–2 days before cooking.

To prepare: remove from pods.

To cook: as green beans, although it is the bean itself that is the main vegetable. When the pods are very soft and young they can be prepared as runner beans and cooked. All other details are as green beans except they are not obtainable as A.F.D. vegetable.

Haricot and butter bean

These are obtainable dried, and need prolonged soaking then cooking, which is really not suitable for a small 'bedsitter' kitchen. They can also be bought in cans, the contents are just heated.

Haricot beans in tomato sauce are a general favourite and, like all beans, an excellent source of protein. They are popularly known as 'baked beans'.

Bean and cheese bake

cooking appliance : oven

Put a layer of sliced cheese in a small oven-proof dish then the contents of a small can of baked beans, cover with another slice of cheese and bake for approximately 20 minutes near the top of a hot oven (425–450°F., Gas Mark 6–7).

To vary :

Bean and bacon bake: as above but put a rasher of bacon, cut into neat pieces, on top of the cheese.

Bean, ham and egg bake

cooking appliance : oven

Mix 2 oz. cooked or canned ham, preferably cut in 1 slice then in neat fingers, with the baked beans.

Heat for 15 minutes, remove from the oven. Break an egg on top and return to the oven for 5 minutes for a lightly set egg or 7–8 minutes for a firmer egg.

Top with a little grated cheese if wished.

Bean and cheese casserole

cooking appliance : boiling ring,
　　　　　　　　　　grill (optional)

Make a white sauce with 1 oz. margarine or butter, as page 74.

Add the contents of a small can of haricot, broad or butter beans. Heat for a few minutes then add 4 oz. grated Cheddar cheese.

Tip into a casserole, top with sliced tomato and a little extra grated cheese.

Brown under the grill if desired. This serves one or two people.

See also Hasty Cassoulet, page 60.

Stuffed pepper, pages 69 and 91.

Bean shoots

In addition to the beans above, you may also like to buy canned bean shoots (the Chinese variety of vegetable). These can be incorporated in Chinese dishes, see page 56 or heated to serve as a separate and interesting vegetable. They are particularly good as an accompaniment to fish dishes.

Beetroot

Beetroot is sold freshly cooked or uncooked. Since the latter takes a long time to boil, it is wiser to purchase the former. These are sold singly, although they will then be weighed to determine the price. One small beetroot (4 oz.) serves 1 or 2 portions.

When fresh: cooked beetroot should look firm and never 'slimy'. Store for a limited time only, 1 day at the most. If buying prepacked beetroot, remove the topping when you get this home to prevent perspiring.

To prepare: remove skin and slice or dice.

To cook: beetroot makes an excellent cooked vegetable. Dice or slice after peeling and heat in either a knob of margarine or butter or in a small amount of cream from the top of the milk, season well.

To serve: cold in salads, tossed in oil and vinegar, or hot as above.

New way to serve: with apple in salad.

Another way to buy beetroot:

Canned beetroot is easily obtained and very good indeed. When opening a can you may find it too much for one person, although small sizes are sold, so I would suggest you use half the can for a hot vegetable and the other half in a salad or for Borsch as page 20. Canned beetroot, well drained, takes the place of cooked beetroot in all dishes.

Broccoli

This vegetable has become much more popular due to the excellent frozen broccoli.

To prepare: as cauliflower, dividing the vegetable into neat pieces and cooking to keep the heads intact. If broken, the flowers are wasted by falling in the cooking water.

To cook: frozen broccoli should be cooked carefully according to the packet.

To serve: topped with a little butter or with a mock Hollandaise sauce as below.

Mock Hollandaise sauce

cooking appliance: boiling ring

This is enough to top sufficient broccoli for 2 portions.

Put 3 tablespoons mayonnaise or salad cream into a basin, stand this over a container of very hot but not boiling water. Add an egg and whisk sharply until a thickened mixture. Serve hot.

Brussels sprouts

These are an excellent vegetable to buy, except for the strong smell when cooking. Allow 4 oz. per person. You can store for 2 days before cooking although they are much better when fresh.

When fresh: firm, tight and green. The open sprout is more wasteful.

To prepare: remove any outer old leaves, mark a cross in the bottom of the stem.

To cook: as cabbage, allow approximately 5–8 minutes for firm sprouts.

To serve: topped with a little margarine or butter.

New ways to serve: topped with a cheese sauce, grated cheese, grilled bacon.

Another way to buy Brussels sprouts

Easily obtainable as frozen sprouts, which are small and tender and smell less in cooking than when fresh.

Cabbage

Cabbages are cheap vegetables but unfortunately they smell most unpleasant when cooking. Read the comments on page 63.

Allow approximately 4 oz. of cabbage per person. If you buy a little cabbage you should have part cooked and part raw in coleslaw, page 71. Cook as soon as possible after buying.

When fresh: firm and green.

To prepare: shred as finely as possible to hasten cooking time.

To cook: in boiling, salted water for approximately 3–5 minutes for a crisp texture.

To serve: topped with butter, cheese sauce or cold in salads.

New way to serve: shredded cabbage can be added to a vegetable soup, to make it like the Italian Minestrone.

Cabbage is only obtainable fresh.

Carrot

Price of carrots will vary tremendously as to whether they are young, new carrots sold in bunches with green leaves, or the older carrot. Allow 2–3 oz. carrots per person. You can store for several days before cooking; older carrots even longer.

When fresh: firm, unblemished, golden colour.

To prepare: scrape new carrots but peel old carrots. Slice or cook whole or grate for speedy cooking.

To cook: in boiling salted water until tender, i.e. 10 minutes for sliced young carrots, 15–20 minutes sliced old carrots, longer for whole carrots.

To serve: toss in margarine or butter, topped with cheese sauce. They are particularly good in brown sauce.

Brown sauce: make as the white sauce on page 74, but use $\frac{1}{4}$ pint water and $\frac{1}{2}$ a beef stock cube in place of the milk.

New ways to serve: grated and added to tomato sauce, see page 75. Grated and added to a cheese sauce as a topping for fish.

Grated and added to salads.

Other ways to buy carrots

Obtainable frozen as part of mixed frozen vegetables or carrots and peas, canned.

Cauliflower

Another vegetable that can make excellent meals, but you should ventilate the room after cooking as the smell lingers. One small cauliflower is enough for 2 portions. You can store for 1 day before cooking. A stale cauliflower is unpleasantly strong smelling.

When fresh: a white, unblemished head and green leaves.

To prepare: cut away outside leaves and stalks. Either cook whole or divided into sprigs (flowerets).

To cook: in boiling, salted water with the white head down in the water. Small sprigs take 5–8 minutes. A whole small cauliflower 15–20 minutes.

To serve: topped with butter, cheese sauce, grated cheese, hard-boiled egg sauce, see page 74.

New ways to serve: sprig the cauliflower and dip each sprig in mayonnaise then roll in a little grated Parmesan cheese. This is excellent with hard-boiled egg salad.

Cook the cauliflower lightly and serve with a tomato purée, made by simmering fresh or canned tomatoes.

Another way to buy cauliflower

Cauliflower is frozen but generally in rather large quantities.

Celeriac

This is an unusual root of celery.

To prepare: peel and dice.

To cook: in boiling, well-seasoned water for 15 to 20 minutes.

To serve: as celery or grate and serve raw.

Celery

This is an excellent vegetable to have raw. I am not giving details for cooking this, although it may be boiled, it may be also diced and added to stews. The canned variety is so good for heating that it is a better purchase for this purpose. The smallest can, however, will serve two to three people. Heat as directed and serve with melted butter, cheese sauce, page 74, or tomato sauce, page 75.

Chicory

This white root, which in some countries is called endive, is generally eaten raw. It is a good buy as you can purchase one head only.

To cook: in boiling, salted water for 10 minutes until tender.

To serve: with melted butter or cheese sauce.

Corn on the cob

This makes an excellent vegetable or even an hors d'oeuvre. Allow 1 corn on the cob per person. It can be kept 1 or 2 days before cooking.

When fresh: green leaves, unwrinkled corn.

To prepare: strip away the green leaves.

To cook: put into boiling, unsalted water. Simmer steadily for nearly 10 minutes, add a little salt and cook for a further 1 to 2 minutes.

To serve: with melted butter.

New ways to serve: the corn kernels may be added to stews, a cheese sauce or put into eggs when scrambling.

Other ways to buy corn on the cob

Canned as creamed corn, i.e. in sauce or corn kernels often mixed with red pepper. Frozen – by itself, on the cob; as kernels or part of mixed vegetables.

Courgettes

These are tiny marrows. You may find them given the Italian name of Zucchinis. They are an excellent buy, as 4 oz. is a very adequate portion for one person and far better when you live alone than buying a marrow. They can be stored for 2 or 3 days.

When fresh: firm and green.

To prepare: cut off the extreme ends, wash and dry but do not peel.

To cook: cut into $\frac{1}{2}$ inch slices. Cook in boiling, salted water for approximately 8 to 10 minutes.

To serve: with melted butter.

New ways to serve: coated and fried as aubergines or simply cooked gently in a saucepan in a rather generous amount of margarine or butter.

Courgettes are only obtainable fresh.

Cucumber

Although this is normally considered a salad vegetable you will find it used in a number of ways in this book, e.g. page 37 and page 89. This is very practical when you are cooking for one or two people, as you do not waste the cucumber.

To keep cucumber fresh, fill a cup or jar with cold water and put one end in this.

Endive

This is the curly looking lettuce which lasts rather better than lettuce, so is a good buy.

Garlic

This may be something you need to avoid in a bedsitter. You can use garlic salt quite liberally.

Leek

This is far less strong smelling than onions and can be used instead. One to 2 large leeks are sufficient for 1 serving, although you will be charged by weight.

When fresh: firm white base, topped with pale green.

To prepare: wash very well between the folds as they can be extremely dirty. Split lengthways or slice.

To cook: in made-up dishes in place of onion or boiling, salted water.

New ways to serve: cooked leek is delicious topped with mayonnaise in a salad. You may also use raw shredded leeks in salads.

Leeks are only obtainable fresh.

Lettuce

This may be a difficult vegetable to buy for one person, as it deteriorates very quickly, but you can sometimes buy lettuce hearts or halved lettuce in large shops. There is a variety of lettuce from which to choose if you are entertaining, and can use a larger size. A few of the varieties are:

Cos: good crisp texture, a long lettuce.

Webb's Wonder: a very crisp texture, keeps well, not unlike a cabbage in appearance.

Round lettuce: the usual type.

To store lettuce without a refrigerator:

DO NOT wash the lettuce, put into a saucepan with a tightly fitting lid, it keeps for several days. You can take off as many leaves as you want and just wash these, dry them and use.

To prepare: wash in cold water, shake dry in kitchen paper or a tea cloth. Do not over handle.

There are so many ways in which lettuce is used in salads and similar dishes that recipes are unnecessary.

Mushrooms

These are one of the most useful of vegetables when you live alone. They give flavour and cook quickly. Allow 2 to 4 oz. for a good portion. Store as short a time as possible before cooking.

When fresh: firm, tight and whitish upper surface. When wrinkled they are stale.

To prepare: good mushrooms do not need skinning. You retain some flavour if you leave the skins on.

To cook: fry in a little butter or as in various recipes.

To serve: as a vegetable or on buttered toast.

Other ways to buy mushrooms

These are not commercially frozen although they freeze extremely well. Canned mushrooms are easily available and very good. Unusual varieties of mushrooms, Chinese or Italian, are dried. Follow the directions and add to various dishes, where required.

Onion

Most people would regard an onion as an essential vegetable for flavouring. They do present problems of smell. Always prepare onions in cold water if you can, to minimise the smell. If you lay a slice of stale bread over a pan in which onions are cooking, the bread absorbs a great deal of the smell. Allow 1 onion per person. I am not treating onions as a vegetable in this book for the reasons given above. It is, however, an excellent idea to buy a jar of small pickled onions or tiny cocktail onions and when a recipe requires an onion use a pickled onion instead. Obviously the flavour varies very slightly.

Another way to buy onions

Dehydrated onion is in the form of tiny pieces of dried onion and is very useful in cooking. Follow the directions on the packet to make the pieces soft enough to use.

Parsnip, turnip and swede

These can be added to stews or cooked the same way as potatoes or carrots.

Peas

These are a most useful vegetable since they provide additional protein. You will need to buy 8 oz. of fresh peas to give 1 portion. You can store them for 1 or 2 days before cooking.

When fresh: firm, green pods, that feel well filled.

To prepare: break the pod and remove the peas.

To cook: in boiling, salted water until tender. A sprig of fresh mint or pinch of dried mint plus a pinch of sugar makes a great improvement in the flavour.

To serve: topped with a little butter or margarine.

New ways to serve: I have used frozen peas since they are the most usual form today.

With orange: use no water in the pan, tip the frozen peas into a saucepan with about 1 oz. butter or margarine, the grated rind and juice of 1 orange.

With butter and herbs: use no water, simply cook the frozen peas with butter, herbs and seasoning. Use chopped fresh mint and parsley to flavour.

Other ways to buy peas

There are three varieties of canned peas, the tiny petits pois, garden peas or the cheaper, rather less tender, processed peas. Simply heat. With frozen peas you can choose between petits pois and ordinary peas. Cook as directed. Although cheap dried peas that need prolonged soaking and cooking are available, the A.F.D. peas, which need no soaking, are an excellent buy as you can help yourself to the quantity you need.

Peppers

This is a vegetable that has the other name of capsicum. Peppers are most useful to add to dishes and use in salads. One green or red pepper is a generous portion for one person. Peppers can be stored 1 or 2 days before using.

To prepare: cut 1 slice from the pepper and then pull out the centre core and seeds. Discard these, then slice the flesh neatly.

To cook: either fry in a little butter until tender or boil in salted water for 5–6 minutes.

To serve: eat raw, or as above. Peppers may be stuffed.

New ways to serve:

Stuffed peppers: cut the pepper lengthways,

remove and discard the core and seeds. Boil in salted water for 5 minutes only. Drain and stuff with:

a baked beans topped with grated cheese.
b filling as aubergines, page 64.
c flaked tuna fish or salmon.

Put a very little butter on top of each of the fillings and bake as aubergines, page 65, or refer to page 91.

Other ways to buy peppers

Red peppers are canned in large and small sizes. The pulp of canned pepper is much softer than that of fresh pepper. Canned peppers are excellent in stews or chopped and added to the eggs in an omelette.

Potatoes

Potatoes are vegetables you can buy in various forms as well as fresh. If you purchase by weight, the amount you buy can depend on personal need. You can store potatoes in a cool place for some time before you cook them, but only a day or so in a warm room.

When fresh: new potatoes have skins that rub off easily. Old potatoes are firm and not wrinkled.

To prepare: new potatoes – scrape away skin, old potatoes – peel. Both may be cooked in their skins to retain flavour. In this case, just scrub the outside well.

To cook:

Boiling: in boiling, salted water until tender for about 20 minutes.

Frying: slice, fry in hot fat in the frying pan for 6–8 minutes.

Bake: prick large old potatoes and cook in their jackets for approximately 1 hour in a moderately hot oven.

You can boil potatoes in their jackets and stuff as below – the skin is not crisp.

Roast: in hot fat in a hot oven for approximately 50 minutes to 1 hour.

New ways to serve:

Cheese potatoes: boil and strain potatoes, mash (or use dehydrated potatoes), add a little milk, knob of butter and some grated cheese. This is excellent with cold meat.

Potato cakes: form mashed potatoes into neat cakes, roll in seasoned flour and fry in hot

fat until crisp and brown. They are excellent for breakfast.

For extra flavour add: a little grated cheese, chopped, fried bacon or herbs and/or pinch curry powder.

Sauté potatoes: slice cooked or canned potatoes and fry in a little hot fat.

Scalloped potatoes: slice raw potatoes very thinly. Put into a dish with seasoning and enough milk to cover, top with a small amount of butter and bake slowly until tender; do not cover the dish. 8 oz. peeled potatoes and about ½ pint milk take 1¼ hours in a slow to very moderate oven (300–325°F., Gas Mark 2–3).

Stuffed potatoes: halve baked potatoes or potatoes boiled in their jackets. Take out the pulp of the potato, mash with seasoning and a little butter or margarine then add:

a little grated cheese.
b flaked cooked or canned fish, especially anchovies.
c diced cooked meat.
d a few canned kidneys.

Reheat after filling.

Other ways to buy potatoes

New potatoes are obtainable in cans, heat and serve as freshly boiled potatoes. Frozen potatoes are available in various forms, e.g. potatoes croquettes – heat through in the oven or in a frying pan in a small amount of hot fat or on a plate over a pan of hot water. Do not cover when heating. There are also chipped potatoes and sliced potatoes. These are partly cooked before being frozen, so the frying period is very short.

Dehydrated potato makes mashed potato very easily. The flavour may be varied by adding a little grated cheese or chopped parsley. Dehydrated potato is also very good for thickening liquids in a stew, see page 58.

Note:

Sweet potatoes (red skinned and rather large) can be cooked as ordinary potatoes and make a pleasant change.

They are only obtainable fresh and are still rather rare.

Radish

Radishes are usually eaten in a salad.

If you have any left over, then add to a stew to take the place of turnips.

Spinach

An excellent vegetable which is rich in iron, so essential to the diet. Allow at least 8 oz. per person as it shrinks in cooking. Do not store at all.

When fresh: firm and green, not limp in any way.

To prepare: wash very well in cold water.

To cook: with very little water in the pan, add a little salt. Cook until tender 12–15 minutes, then strain.

To serve: with a little butter or blended with cream, a shake of pepper and grating of nutmeg if wished.

Other ways to buy spinach

Canned spinach is used as freshly cooked spinach and heated.

With frozen spinach, cook as directed.

Tomato

One of the most versatile of vegetables and rich in Vitamin C. Eat raw or cooked. Allow 1 or 2 per person. You can store for 1 or 2 days.

When fresh: firm and red.

To prepare: slice or serve whole. To skin, put for ½ minute in boiling water, lift out and put in cold water; or insert a fine skewer in the tomato and hold for a few seconds over the gas ring. The heat of the flame causes the skin to split, making it easy to remove.

To cook: as recipes in the book.

To serve: sliced with a little French dressing. If wished, chill before serving.

Other ways to buy tomatoes

Canned tomatoes are plum shaped and have a much better flavour than fresh tomatoes in cooking. Tomato purée, very concentrated, may be purchased in tubes. Add a little to dishes for extra flavour.

Watercress

A wonderful salad vegetable which is bought in bunches or buy 4 oz. in weight. Eat with hot or cold dishes. Use when fresh, although it can be kept with the stalks in a cup or jar of cold water for 1 day.

When fresh: firm and green, not limp.

To prepare: wash in cold water, remove bottom of stalks.

To serve: uncooked.

Remember you can buy boxes of ordinary cress that is growing and you cut off as much as you need at a time.

Salads

Remember a salad is as good an accompaniment to hot dishes as to cold. Here are some suggestions:

Beetroot and apple salad
Blend grated or chopped cooked beetroot and raw apple.

Bean salad
Toss cooked green beans in oil and vinegar and serve with sliced tomato.

Carrot salad
Grate raw peeled carrots coarsely. Serve on watercress with cheese, mixed with mayonnaise and chopped nuts.

Coleslaw
An excellent way of using cabbage. Shred young cabbage leaves very finely (Brussels sprouts could be used), mix with mayonnaise and with:

a chopped nuts
b chopped apple
c little canned pineapple.

Cheese salad
Use a variety of cheeses in salads with nuts or with fresh or canned fruit.

Egg salad
Hard-boil or scramble eggs and use in salads (or lettuce, watercress or mustard and cress) with:

a cream cheese
b sardines or anchovies
c mayonnaise flavoured with paprika, curry powder or tomato ketchup.

Orange salad
Cut away the peel from oranges to remove pith

too and divide orange into neat segments. Serve with lettuce. Remember most other fruits are excellent in salads.

Potato salad

Mix sliced, cooked or canned potatoes with mayonnaise and:

a chopped gherkins

b chopped cocktail onions and parsley.

You can also buy canned potato salad.

Russian salad

Mix drained, cooked or canned mixed vegetables with mayonnaise.

Avocado and cream cheese salad

no cooking

you will need for 1 serving :

1 small avocado pear	1 teaspoon lemon juice or vinegar
2 oz. cream cheese or cheese spread	
1 tablespoon thin cream, top of the milk or mayonnaise	**to garnish:**
seasoning	tomato watercress

1 Halve the avocado pear lengthways, remove the stone.

2 Take out the pulp carefully so you keep the skin intact, this is not difficult to do if the avocado pear is ripe – see page 16 for the way to judge this.

3 Put the pulp of the avocado pear into a basin and mash this with a fork.

4 Add the cheese, cream, seasoning (use very little seasoning when mayonnaise is chosen instead of cream), then add the lemon juice or vinegar – this helps to keep the pear flesh a good colour as well as flavouring the mixture.

5 Pile the soft mixture into the two halves of the pear and serve on a plate with sliced tomato and watercress.

Note :

This is very filling and slightly rich, so should be served with plenty of crispbread or fresh bread and followed by a plain dessert. If preferred, make this into 2 small portions and use more tomatoes.

There are more interesting recipes using avocado pears on pages 16 to 17. As you will see, avocado pears make a delightful and special hors d'oeuvre.

Cooking with pasta

Pasta is the name given to foods such as spaghetti and macaroni. There is a wonderful selection in shops today.

Pasta is an excellent basis for dishes when you have limited cooking facilities, for you can prepare most satisfying meals with just one boiling ring.

To make a meal from pasta using one saucepan and boiling ring

You can cook the pasta, strain this through a sieve or colander, then rinse it in cold water so it does not become sticky. You then make the chosen sauce in the saucepan used for cooking the pasta and when the sauce is ready, add the pasta. Reheat, then serve.

To make a meal from pasta using two saucepans and boiling rings

You can cook the pasta and sauce simultaneously. Check the recipe to see which takes the longer cooking, for pasta is spoiled if overcooked. If you can cook the sauce and the pasta at the same time, there is no need to rinse the pasta. Drain the pasta, put into the serving dish or on the plates, top with the sauce and serve.

To reheat pasta

If you cook too much pasta do not waste it, rinse in cold water, then put it into a basin and cover with foil or greaseproof paper.

When you wish to reheat it, put for a few minutes in boiling salted water. Drain, then toss in a little butter or margarine or simply tip into the hot sauce and heat.

To serve pasta as a vegetable

Pasta makes an excellent substitute for potatoes as a vegetable; boil and drain. There is no need to rinse it if using at once, toss in a little margarine or butter in the saucepan, then top with a shake of paprika or chopped parsley.

Choosing pasta

Obviously with limited storage space you cannot stock up on all types of pasta, but it is interesting to know about some of the shapes and types available.

These are the types you can use as a vegetable or with a sauce.

Capellini:	almost as fine as fideline.
Ditali:	largest size tubes of cut macaroni.
Farfalle:	bows in all sizes.
Fettuccine:	long, wide egg noodles.
Fideline:	finest spaghetti. Comes 'nested'.
Fusilli:	twisted macaroni with hole through it. Considered supreme achievement of spaghetti worker's art.
Lasagne:	ribbons of pasta, used in baked dishes.
Linguine:	flat, ribbon-like spaghetti, often served with fish.
Maccheroni: (macaroni)	generic term for larger pasta varieties. Outside Italy, the name is commonly used to describe the thickish, pipe-stem tubes of pasta.
Spaghetti:	long thin rounds used with sauces.
Verdi:	'green' pastas which have been mixed with spinach. One has, for example, lasagna verdi.
Vermicelli:	long, thin, round pasta used in soups.

It must be stressed that these are only a selection of the pasta you can obtain.

More specialised types of pasta

Cannelloni:	these are large tubes of pasta which are boiled, drained, stuffed, topped with a sauce and baked. You may be able to buy frozen cannelloni in a sauce, for reheating.
Ravioli:	this is another form of stuffed pasta and is sold in cans. The contents of the can are heated as directed. As the filling is of meat, this makes a substantial dish.

Again there are other types of filled pasta but the two above are the most usual and useful for your menus.

To cook pasta

It is important to allow sufficient water when cooking pasta for it must move around in the pan, so preventing it becoming sticky or sticking to the bottom of the saucepan. It is always difficult to suggest quantities of pasta, as each person varies tremendously in the amount they can eat, but 1–1½ oz. is sufficient for a small portion or to serve as a vegetable. If pasta is your main dish however you may wish to increase this to 2–2½ oz. per person.

If you are very fond of pasta remember you can cook a double amount and just reheat it on another occasion.

Remember, if you are watching your weight that pasta is a carbohydrate food and is high in calories.

To cook pasta, allow 1 pint water to each 2 oz. pasta. Bring the water to the boil, adding a very good pinch salt (as desired). Add the pasta and cook until tender. Pasta varies in cooking time but you can test by pressing a piece with a fork and if it feels tender then strain.

Spaghetti takes approximately 12 minutes to become just tender. Finer pasta would take a little less time and larger pasta a little longer.

Long spaghetti

Most pasta is easy to put into the boiling water except long spaghetti which is rather more difficult, so this is the method to employ:

1 Bring water to the boil, add salt to taste – do not over-salt, you can always add a little more at the end of the cooking time.
2 Hold the bundle of spaghetti in your hand and lower one end into the water, allow this to cook for about ½–1 minute when it will soften, then twist the spaghetti so more goes into the boiling water. You may have to wait ½–1 minute before adding all the spaghetti.
3 After the spaghetti has been cooking for 3–4 minutes lift in the water to separate the 'strands'.
4 Cook until tender, drain and serve.

Ways to serve pasta

There are many classic and quite elaborate

recipes using pasta, but the following are easy to prepare.

With grated cheese. Drain pasta, return to the pan and toss in butter then serve with plenty of grated Cheddar, Parmesan or other cheese.

With cheese sauce

Many recipes include a cheese sauce as well as pasta. The usual method of making a cheese sauce is to first make a white sauce and *then* add the cheese, but when time is limited there are other methods you can use as below.

White sauce – blending method

cooking time : 10 minutes
cooking appliance : boiling ring

you will need for 1–2 servings :

½ oz. flour or 2 level   ¼ pint milk
   teaspoons cornflour   ½ oz. butter or
seasoning   margarine

1 Blend the flour with the seasoning and a quarter of the milk, stirring with a wooden spoon until you have a smooth paste.
2 Bring the rest of the milk to the boil, pour slowly over the flour mixture, stirring all the time to prevent lumps forming.
3 Tip the sauce back into the saucepan and stir over a low heat until the mixture boils. Cook for 3 minutes, stirring all the time, adding the butter or margarine towards the end of the time.
4 Taste, and if necessary, season again.
The above is the simpler method of making a sauce, the recipe below the more classic method.

White sauce – 'roux' method

cooking time : 10 minutes
cooking appliance : boiling ring

you will need for 1–2 servings :

½ oz. margarine   ¼ pint milk
   or butter   seasoning
½ oz. flour or 2 level
   teaspoons cornflour

1 Heat the margarine or butter in a small saucepan.
2 Remove from the heat and stir in the flour with a wooden spoon.
3 Return this mixture of fat and flour, called 'roux', to a low heat. Cook for 2–3 minutes, stirring well. Take care that the 'roux' does not change colour; cook only until it is dry and crumbly.
4 Remove the pan from the heat once again, gradually stir in the milk.
5 Add the liquid sufficiently slowly so that it blends into the 'roux' and the mixture keeps perfectly smooth.
6 Add the salt and pepper and put the sauce back again over the heat. Bring to the boil, stirring all the time.
7 When the sauce has come to the boil, lower the heat and continue cooking for 3 minutes.
8 Taste and, if necessary, add more salt and pepper.

To make a cheese sauce

Add 2 oz. grated or diced cheese (Cheddar, Parmesan, Gruyère or other cooking cheese – see page 27) to the sauce *when it has thickened* and heat for a few minutes only. Do not overcook when the cheese is added.

Evaporated milk cheese sauce

Put ¼ pint unsweetened evaporated milk into a basin, stand over a pan of hot water. Heat, add seasoning and 2–3 oz. grated or diced cheese (cooking variety). Continue heating until the cheese has melted.

Mayonnaise cheese sauce

Put 4 tablespoons mayonnaise and 4 tablespoons milk into basin over a pan of hot water. Heat, add seasoning and 2–3 oz. grated or diced cheese (cooking variety). Heat until the cheese melts.

Pasta with anchovy sauce

Cook the pasta, make the white sauce, add up to ½ can chopped anchovies to each ¼ pint sauce. Be sparing with salt in cooking the pasta. Serve on the pasta and top with grated cheese.

Pasta with egg sauce

Cook the pasta, boil 1 or 2 eggs until hard, shell and chop.

Make the white or any of the cheese sauces, add the eggs. Top the pasta with this sauce.

Spaghetti alla marinara

This is an excellent mixture of fish and spaghetti. There are various methods of preparing the dish – this is one way:

cooking time: 15 minutes
cooking appliance: boiling ring

you will need for 2 servings:

4 oz. spaghetti or other pasta	seasoning

for the sauce:

1 oz. butter	small can tuna
small can tomatoes	$\frac{1}{2}$ can anchovies
seasoning	

to serve:

1 oz. cheese

1 Boil spaghetti in salted or well-seasoned water as page 73. When tender, drain.
2 Heat the butter with the tomatoes, season well, add flaked tuna and chopped anchovies.
3 Pile over spaghetti, top with grated cheese.
   To vary:
   With ham: add chopped, cooked ham instead of tuna.
   With other fish: add prawns, flaked salmon or other fish instead of tuna.

Pasta with tomato sauce

The easiest tomato sauce is made by heating a can of tomatoes and seasoning well or by adding:

a brown sugar and garlic salt.
b a chopped rasher of bacon.
c a chopped or grated onion and a little chopped or grated apple or carrot.
d pinch curry powder, dry mustard and few drops of Worcestershire sauce.

A more interesting tomato sauce is:
cooking time: 35 minutes
cooking appliance: boiling ring

you will need for 2–4 servings:

1 oz. butter or margarine	$\frac{1}{2}$ pint water or water and 1 chicken stock cube
1 small onion	
1 small rasher bacon	good pinch salt
8 oz. ripe tomatoes	shake pepper
$\frac{1}{2}$ oz. flour or $\frac{1}{4}$ oz. cornflour	good pinch sugar

1 Heat the butter or margarine and toss the finely chopped or grated onion and finely chopped bacon in this for several minutes. Do not allow to become brown in colour.
2 Skin and chop the tomatoes, add to the onion and bacon mixture, then cook for 2 minutes, stirring well. Remove from the heat.
3 Blend the flour with the stock and stir into the sauce with the salt, pepper, and sugar.
4 Bring to the boil, stirring well.
5 When the sauce has thickened slightly and becomes clear, lower the heat, cover the pan and simmer gently for 25 minutes. Stir from time to time.
6 Sieve and reheat the sauce if you wish.
   Taste and add more seasoning if required.

Spaghetti with meat sauce

The easiest meat sauce is to open a can of stewed steak and heat this, breaking the meat into smaller pieces. This can be improved by:

a frying a chopped or grated onion in $\frac{1}{2}$–1 oz. butter or fat before adding the meat.
b frying 1–2 oz. sliced mushrooms and/or a skinned chopped tomato and/or a chopped onion in 1 oz. butter or fat before adding the meat.
c adding pinch herbs, little curry powder, shake garlic salt, few drops Worcestershire sauce.
   A more savoury meat sauce is given below:

Meat sauce

cooking time: $1\frac{1}{4}$ hours
cooking appliance: boiling ring

you will need for 2–4 servings:

1 onion	$\frac{1}{2}$ pint water, 1 beef stock cube
1–2 tomatoes	
1 oz. fat	8 oz. minced beef
$\frac{1}{2}$ oz. flour	seasoning

1 Peel onion and skin tomatoes, and cut into small pieces.
2 Fry the onion for 3 minutes in the hot fat, taking care it does not become too brown.
3 Add the tomatoes and cook for a further 2 minutes.
4 Gradually stir in the flour, away from the heat. Cook over a low heat for 2–3 minutes, stirring all the time.
5 Add the liquid slowly, following the same

procedure as when adding milk in a white sauce.

6 Bring to the boil and cook until you have a slightly thickened sauce.

7 Add the meat, stir this well to break it into small pieces. Add the seasoning.

8 Cook in a covered saucepan for 1 hour, stirring from time to time to keep the meat mixture smooth.

9 Taste and reseason if necessary.

Note:

A pinch of mixed herbs may be added, or a finely chopped carrot cooked with the onion and tomatoes.

To vary:

a Add a little chopped green or red pepper.

b Flavour with herbs.

c Add 1–2 oz. chopped mushrooms at stage 8.

Using canned pasta

Canned spaghetti and macaroni are extremely useful as filling foods to serve with meat and fish.

There is a certain amount of cheese in some canned pasta, but you add to the protein content of your meal if you top the heated pasta with more cheese, an egg or have it with bacon or other meat or fish. Remember canned pasta is well cooked, so do not over-heat otherwise it becomes too soft.

If more convenient, you can serve canned spaghetti in the recipes in the preceding pages e.g.

Spaghetti alla marinara

Make the sauce and when hot either add the canned spaghetti and heat with the sauce or heat the canned spaghetti and sauce separately. The same procedure can be followed with the meat sauce, but if using canned spaghetti in tomato sauce omit the tomatoes from the meat sauce, recipe on page 75.

Cooking savoury rice dishes

Rice is an excellent food to cook for savoury dishes.

When shopping choose long grain rice, often called Patna rice, although it now comes from various countries. There is also available quick cooking rice of various kinds. If using this you will find cooking instructions on the packet, follow these and use in the recipes. I have given the cooking time for ordinary rice.

You will also find 'cook in the bag' rice, which means you do not dirty a saucepan.

There are many ways of boiling rice, most of them quite satisfactory, but in the method I have given below you do not need to rinse the rice after cooking and yet every grain keeps separate.

To boil rice

In this method you allow exactly double the amount of water to the amount of rice, e.g. if you use 2 oz. rice then you use 4 fluid oz. water. If you use $\frac{1}{2}$ cup of rice then you use 1 cup of water. The size of the cup is immaterial, providing you use the *same* cup for both rice and water.

The quantity of rice per person varies a great deal. I have allowed 2 tablespoons (approximately 2 oz.), but you may need more. Remember, you can reheat rice.

cooking time: 16 minutes
cooking appliance: boiling ring

you will need for 1 serving:
2 oz. long grain rice   salt to taste
4 fluid oz. water*

*This is nearly 6 average tablespoons.

1 Wash the rice unless using the pre-packed, ready cleaned rice. If you wash the rice, cook at once.

2 Put into the saucepan with the cold water and a little salt.

3 Bring as quickly as possible to the boil.

4 Stir with a fork, put a lid on the pan and lower the heat and simmer for 15 minutes, when all the liquid should have been absorbed.

To serve as a vegetable

Blend with a small knob of butter or margarine and season well.

To serve in a salad

Blend with a little mayonnaise (while the rice is hot if possible) then cool and add:

a any left-over cooked peas or other vegetables

b grated raw carrot and/or chopped chicory

c any small pieces of left-over meat or fish.

If you can add the mayonnaise while the rice is hot, you will find it absorbs the flavour better.

To heat left-over rice

Cover the rice with foil when you store it, so it does not become too hard on top.

To reheat

Either heat 1 tablespoon water (for 2 oz. rice) and when boiling put the rice in this and boil until the water has gone or heat ½ oz. butter (for 2 oz. rice) and toss the cooked rice in this.

To fry rice

Ideally when you fry rice it should be slightly under cooked, but you can use well-dried, left-over rice for this purpose. Simply heat about 1 tablespoon oil or fat (for 2 oz. rice) in a frying pan and cook until the rice is golden coloured.

Saffron rice

cooking time: 20 minutes
cooking appliance: boiling ring

you will need for 2 servings:

1 small cup Patna rice*	½–1 oz. butter
2 cups cold water (use the same cup)	1–2 oz. walnuts or almonds
½ level teaspoon salt	
pinch powdered saffron	

*it does not matter about the capacity of the cup, providing the same cup is used for both rice and water.

1 Wash the rice, unless using pre-packed, ready washed rice. If washing the rice in cold water USE at once to prevent it becoming sticky.

2 Tip the rice and water into a large saucepan (one with a tight-fitting lid), add the salt and saffron and bring to the boil, stir once with a fork.

3 Lower the heat, replace the lid and simmer for about 15 minutes *without* stirring or removing the lid.

4 Test the rice by biting a few grains, if not quite tender, or if the liquid is not quite absorbed, replace the lid and cook for a few minutes

longer. When dry and fluffy, remove from the heat.

5 Fork in the butter and chopped nuts and turn onto a serving dish.

To curry rice

cooking time: 20 minutes
cooking appliance: boiling ring

you will need for 2 servings:

4 oz. long grain rice	2 teaspoons curry powder
1 tablespoon oil or 1 oz. butter	½ pint water
1 onion	½ tablespoon sultanas
1 small apple	seasoning

1 Wash the rice unless using pre-packed ready washed rice.

2 Heat the oil or butter and fry the peeled, grated onion and apple for a few minutes, then add the rice and curry powder and cook for 1 minute.

3 Add the water and bring to the boil. Lower the heat and cook for 15 minutes, then stir in sultanas and seasoning to taste. This is excellent hot or cold. If serving cold, you can blend a very little mayonnaise into the rice mixture. Serve it with cheese, cold meat or hard-boiled eggs.

Kedgeree No. 1

cooking time: 14 – 15 minutes
                    or see method
cooking appliance: boiling ring

you will need for 1 serving:

1 egg	½ oz. butter
2 oz. cooked rice	2 tablespoons cream from top of milk
small portion cooked haddock	seasoning

1 Hard-boil, shell and chop the egg.

2 If you have more than one boiling ring you can be cooking the egg in one pan and the kedgeree in a second, which shortens cooking time.

3 Put the rest of the ingredients into a pan, breaking the fish into small portions.

4 Heat gently and put on to a hot plate and top with chopped egg.

Risotto

This Italian word for cooked rice means, to most people, a delicious combination of rice and savoury ingredients. There are many recipes for risotto – some based on vegetables, others on meat or fish. The great advantage of this dish is that you can produce a satisfying meal in one saucepan.

The correct type of rice to use is Italian – which has an almost transparent look when cooked, but long grain could be substituted. Dehydrated soup is suggested in the recipe as it provides stock and onion flavours; use fresh, chopped onion and water and a stock cube if wished.

Vegetable risotto

cooking time : 30 minutes
cooking appliance : boiling ring

you will need for 1 serving :

1 oz. butter or	2 oz. rice
1 tablespoon oil	¼ packet dehydrated
2 oz. mushrooms	onion soup
2 tomatoes	½ pint water
	few canned or cooked
	peas

to serve :

little cheese

1 Heat the butter or oil in a good sized saucepan, toss the sliced mushrooms and skinned, sliced tomatoes in this.
2 Add the rice and turn in the butter or oil mixture, then add the soup powder which has been blended with the water in a basin.
3 Cook steadily in an uncovered pan, stirring from time to time, until the rice has absorbed the liquid, add peas when nearly cooked.
4 Pile on to a hot dish and top with grated cheese.

To vary :

Add a few sultanas or other dried fruit just before the rice is cooked.

Meat risotto : Possibly the best known risotto in this country is the one made with chicken's livers. These are not easy to obtain, some butchers may sell them or they can sometimes be obtained in frozen form. If you cannot buy these (you need 3–4 livers), then buy 4 oz. calf's liver. Dice the liver and add after the rice has been cooking for 10 minutes.

Note :

Seasoning is omitted in the risotto recipe above, as dehydrated onion soup is already well seasoned. You may however like to add a little, so taste before serving.

Fish risotto : Using the same recipe, omit the peas if wished and add 2–4 oz. shell, canned or other fish.

Another form of kedgeree may be made by using this method, adding diced, uncooked smoked haddock at stage 2. Use onion soup for a very savoury **kedgeree** or omit this and cook the rice in milk and water. Top with a chopped hard-boiled egg instead of cheese.

Cold desserts and hot puddings

Cold desserts

There are many desserts you can make in a very short time. If you look around the shelves in a good grocers you will find many instant puddings that simply need the addition of milk. One of the best cold desserts is fruit. Even when you entertain you will find your guests appreciate good fresh fruit, particularly if it is rather special, like berry fruit (raspberries, etc.) or fresh pineapple, or unusual like ugli (cross between an orange and a grapefruit). There are however simple ways in which you can make the common fruit more interesting, see below: All recipes are for 2 people.

Apples

Apples and cream cheese

This is a pleasant combination of sweet and savoury. Cut two very perfect apples into thick slices, do not peel, but remove the core if possible. You can do this with the point of a sharp knife, but if you buy an apple corer it does it much more easily (apple corers are very cheap). Spread the rings of apple with soft cream cheese – you will need 2–3 oz. for 2 people, and top with halved walnuts or dessert dates.

Apple and ice cream whip

Put enough ice cream for two people into a basin. Peel 1 or 2 dessert apples and either chop the fruit finely or grate it into the ice cream.
Pile into glasses and serve at once, topped with flaked almonds or halved, dried walnuts if wished.
A few flaked almonds or chopped walnuts may also be added to the ice cream mixture.

Bananas

Lemon bananas

Slice 2 large firm bananas for each person, and mix with 2 teaspoons lemon juice, 2 teaspoons sugar.
Whisk $\frac{1}{4}$ pint thick cream until it just holds its shape – do not over-whisk, then add the bananas. Put into 2 glasses and top with flaked almonds.

Banana split

Put a portion of ice cream on to each dish, top with a whole banana and melted redcurrant jelly, defrosted frozen raspberries or fresh raspberries mashed with a little sugar to make a sauce.
Note:
Choose bananas that are *just* ripe for these desserts and not over-ripe, i.e. the skin should be golden but with few dark brown or black marks.

Oranges

Caramel oranges

This dish is one of the most 'fashionable' of desserts today, where fresh oranges are coated with a caramel sauce. It is not difficult to prepare, it can be done beforehand so is ideal when you entertain. Fresh clemantines (preferably large in size) are also excellent for this. Normally one makes the caramel with sugar and water, but you may have golden syrup in the cupboard so I have given you both methods of preparing the caramel. The quantity of 4 large oranges or the equivalent gives enough for 4 medium servings or 2 very generous ones.

cooking time: few minutes
cooking appliance: boiling ring

you will need for 2–4 servings:

4 large oranges (ask for seedless oranges if possible)
or 6–8 clemantines

for the caramel:

3 oz. sugar – castor, granulated, loaf, but not brown sugar	6 tablespoons water or 3 tablespoons golden syrup with 3 tablespoons water

1 The most difficult part of this recipe is to cut away the orange rind with the white pith. To do this take a really sharp knife and cut into the fruit at the top in a slice, then gradually cut round the fruit. When you do this, hold the orange over the saucepan to be used for the caramel so that no juice is wasted.
2 Put the orange into a serving dish.
3 Put the sugar and 3 tablespoons of the water into the saucepan.
4 Stir over a low heat, until the sugar melts – use a wooden spoon for this if possible.
5 When the sugar has melted allow the caramel to boil steadily until it turns golden brown. Do not leave the caramel during this stage, as it takes only a minute or two for a golden caramel to turn quite dark and when this happens the flavour is spoiled, the sugar and water or syrup will taste bitter.
If using golden syrup do not add any water at this stage, simply allow the syrup to boil slowly until it changes in colour to a very slightly darker golden brown.
6 If using either sugar or syrup, remove the pan from the heat, add the rest of the water. This will sound quite alarming, since the caramel generally 'splutters' violently and may form a fairly solid ball – do not worry, this is quite all right. Put the pan back over the heat and stir until the caramel and water have

blended together. Pour this over the oranges while warm, but allow the syrup to become cold before serving.

To serve: cut the fruit into thick slices and put on to the plates, coated with the sauce.

Melon

A melon is not only an excellent beginning for a meal but also can be turned into a delicious dessert.

Watch the shops to see when melon is at its best and cheapest. You may also find some shops sell portions of melon. A melon is ripe when the flesh 'yields' or feels soft to touch when gently pressed at the stalk end. Melons vary however in the amount the flesh will 'yield' – an Ogen or Charentais feels really very soft all over when ripe but a honeydew (particularly the green variety) is ripe when only the tip is soft. The yellow honeydew and cantaloups should have quite a large circle of soft flesh at the stalk end of the melon.

Two of the best melons to buy for a very special occasion are the Ogen melon or a Charentais. These are small melons and to prepare them you cut across the centre, scoop out the seeds and serve a half to each person. They are however often more expensive than honeydew or cantaloup melons.

Sherry melon

Either cut small melons into halves or cut slices of larger melon, and remove the seeds. Sprinkle a little sweet dry sherry over the melon, leave this for several hours before serving so the sherry penetrates into the fruit. Serve with sugar.

I have given the following recipe for 4 servings as you may find this an ideal dessert for a special party.

Melon with raspberry sauce

no cooking

you will need for 4 servings:

1 medium sized, ripe melon	¼ pint thick cream
12 oz.–1 lb. ripe raspberries plus sugar to taste or 1 packet frozen raspberries	

1 Cut the melon into slices, then remove the seeds and cut the flesh into neat dice.
2 Put into serving dishes or on plates.
3 Mash fresh raspberries with the sugar until they form a sauce. (You will need about 2 tablespoons sugar). If using frozen raspberries allow these to defrost then mash until a sauce. If you are in a hurry put the unopened packet or bag of fruit into a bowl of cold water to hasten defrosting.
4 Stir the cream into the raspberry pulp.
5 Spoon over the melon and serve.
Do not add the sauce until just before serving.

Strawberries

Fresh strawberries, like raspberries, are probably better served just with sugar and cream than in any other way, but if you do wish to give them a very unusual and pleasant flavour, allow them to soak in white wine.

Remove the stalks from 1 lb. fresh firm strawberries. Put on to a flat dish and sprinkle over about a wineglass of white wine. Leave for several hours then serve with sugar and cream.

Pineapple

Fresh pineapple makes one of the best of all desserts and there are times of the year when small pineapples are comparatively inexpensive. A pineapple is at its best when uniformly golden in colour. If it is rather green on the outside, it is not quite ripe. If on the other hand it feels very soft to the touch and there are brownish patches on the skin, it is either over-ripe or bruised.

To prepare fresh pineapple

The pineapple is served in slices, with the skin and centre hard core removed. I find it easier to slice the pineapple before removing the skin.

Cut the pineapple into slices about ¾ inch thick, then cut off the skin with a sharp knife or pair of kitchen scissors – do this over a plate or bowl, so no juice is wasted. Remove the centre core with a sharp knife or use an apple corer. Put the slices of pineapple on serving plates and pour over any juice that may have flowed when peeling.

Serve with sugar and cream, or you can sprinkle the pineapple with a little sherry.

Jelly

To use packet jellies

Your only problem may be to get a jelly to set in a warm living room, but in cold weather or when you have a refrigerator this is no problem. If you are somewhat worried about whether the jelly *will* set, use a little less water than the amount recommended on the packet, i.e. if 1 pint is required, use about 3 tablespoons less. Do not make a habit of this though, as it does produce a rather stiff jelly which is less palatable.

Quantity of jelly to use

You can always use part of a jelly tablet and just return the remainder to the packet, sealing this up tightly to prevent it becoming sticky due to exposure to the air.

I am however giving you the quantity of filling, etc. for a whole jelly, so you will need to divide this.

A milk jelly is both a nutritious and delicious dessert.

Milk jelly

cooking time : few minutes
cooking appliance : boiling ring

you will need for 4 servings :

1 fruit flavoured jelly tablet	¼ pint water ¾ pint cold milk

1 Put the jelly into a basin, breaking it into pieces.
2 Boil the water and pour the boiling water over the jelly, then stir until the jelly has dissolved. If by chance it does not dissolve in this small amount of liquid, stand the basin over a saucepan of boiling water for a short time.
3 Allow the jelly to cool, then add the cold milk, in this way you prevent any possibility of the jelly curdling the milk.
4 Pour into a basin, rinsed out in cold water. Allow to set, then turn out. By rinsing the basin you make sure the jelly comes out easily.

To vary :

Evaporated milk jelly : Use undiluted evaporated milk in place of cold milk.

Cream jelly : Use ½ pint milk and ¼ pint thin cream in place of all milk.

Cherry milk jelly : Open a small can of cherries and pour off the juice, use ¼ pint of this instead of water, and heat in a saucepan. Add just over ½ pint cold milk to jelly and cherries. Do not try and turn this out, just put it into a serving dish to set. Cherries blend well with orange and lemon jelly.

Other canned fruit could be used instead of cherries; try mandarin oranges.

Fruit filled jellies

You can turn an ordinary jelly into a much more interesting dessert, if you add fresh or canned fruit to the jelly. Remember, though, that all fruit is moist and reduce the amount of water used (except for bananas).

If using bananas : use the normal amount of liquid to dissolve the jelly, allow this to cool then add 2–3 sliced bananas to 1 pint of jelly.

If using other fresh fruit : for sliced apples, segments of fresh orange, pieces of melon, segments of fresh peach, etc., allow only ¾ pint to a 1 pint jelly.

NEVER USE FRESH PINEAPPLE IN A JELLY, IT STOPS THE JELLY SETTING.

If using canned fruit : pierce 2 holes in the can of fruit and pour out the liquid. Measure this and add enough water to give ¾ pint. Heat this, add to the jelly and stir until dissolved. Cool then add the well-drained, canned fruit. Either put into a rinsed basin or serving dish to set.

To fill a sponge flan

Most supermarkets and grocers today sell ready prepared sponge flans. Keep these in the polythene wrapping until you are ready to fill them, this keeps the sponge moist. The flans you buy are enough for 4 medium sized portions, so if you wish this for 2 portions only, open the packet, cut off half the flan and return the rest to the packet and seal down at once.

The fillings suggested are for a whole flan – so halve the amounts for a smaller portion.

Chocolate and coffee filling : buy a large block of coffee ice cream and 4 oz. plain chocolate. Put the ice cream into the sponge flan, spreading this out slightly so it makes a good filling for the flan. Break the chocolate into small pieces and put into a basin and stand this over or in a saucepan containing a little water. Add 1 tablespoon water to the chocolate and heat over a low heat until melted. Spoon the hot chocolate over the coffee ice cream just before serving.

Chocolate and pear filling: buy a medium sized can of halved pears and 4 oz. plain chocolate. Open the can of pears and arrange these in the sponge flan. Put the chocolate and 1 tablespoon syrup from the can of pears into the basin and proceed as above.

Ice cream and fruit: fill the flan with vanilla or other flavoured ice cream – you will need a large block for 4 portions. Top with fresh fruit, choose from the following:

a sliced bananas (dipped in lemon juice to keep the slices white),

b segments of canned mandarin orange or segments of fresh oranges,

c fresh, or *well-drained*, canned or defrosted strawberries or raspberries, etc.,

d any other *well-drained*, canned or defrosted, frozen fruit.

Ice cream

To serve ice cream

Ice cream is one of the most popular of desserts today, and since you can buy such a large selection of flavours, it should not become monotonous.

If you have no refrigerator, wrap the ice cream in several thicknesses of newspaper to give insulation, this will keep it firm for several hours if stored in a cool place. If you have a wide necked vacuum flask, put the ice cream in this to keep cool for several hours. It may be kept in the carton or unwrapped, whichever fits in better.

To give new flavour to ice cream

Top with hot chocolate sauce, see page 81.

Top with rose hip syrup or blackcurrant syrup – both are excellent sources of Vitamin C and sufficiently thick to form a syrup.

With fruit: serve with fresh, canned or frozen fruit.

With nuts and chocolate: top with grated or chopped chocolate and chopped nuts.

With redcurrant jelly: top with melted redcurrant jelly mixed with glacé cherries.

Yoghourt

Using yoghourt for simple desserts

Yoghourt has become so readily available that it means you can always have a quick and simple dessert.

a Serve natural yoghourt with sugar and a sprinkling of grated nutmeg, topped with fruit or blended with chopped fresh apple or other fruits in season.

b **With jelly:** dissolve a $\frac{1}{2}$ pint jelly (half a packet) in $\frac{1}{4}$ pint boiling water, cool, then add a carton of natural yoghourt.

c **With nuts:** serve fruit flavoured yoghourt, topped with chopped nuts.

Hot puddings

A hot pudding is not difficult to produce, even for one person, and it gives you an excellent opportunity to 'show off' your cooking skill when you entertain. When time is precious, there are many prepared puddings you can buy.

Ready prepared puddings

Bakers, supermarkets, all sell tarts and small pies made with fruits in season.

There are canned puddings that just need reheating – make these more interesting with quick sauces made by heating canned fruit, fruit purée, jam or redcurrant jelly.

Creamed rice is obtainable in cans and makes an easy, hot pudding.

There are packet puddings for fruit crumbles, and packet and frozen pastry.

Fruit pies

If you have facilities for baking you can easily make fruit pies. Choose either frozen short or puff pastry and use canned pie fillings, canned fruit or fresh fruit.

Allow the pastry you buy to defrost sufficiently so it can be rolled out. If you have no rolling pin, a dry empty milk bottle or jam jar could be used instead.

The packets of frozen pastry each make enough for 4 helpings so you will need a good sized can of pie filling or canned fruit or about 1 lb. prepared fresh fruit (this means the weight when peeled and prepared).

Put the fruit into the pie dish, add enough sugar to sweeten fresh fruit and 1–2 tablespoons water, or use orange juice with rhubarb or water and lemon juice with apples. If using canned fruit, strain off the surplus syrup and do not sweeten. Canned pie fillings are ready to use.

Roll out the pastry; if using a proper pie dish, cut narrow strips to go round the moistened rim of the dish. Put in the fruit as instructed above, cover with the rest of the pastry. Seal the edges well. Bake a pie with short crust, in the centre of a moderately hot to hot oven (400–425°F., Gas Mark 5–6) for 20 minutes, then lower the heat to moderate for a further 20 minutes, or until the pastry is golden brown. If using puff pastry, bake the pie for about 15 minutes in the centre of a very hot oven (450–475°F., Gas Mark 7-8) then lower the heat to very moderate and bake for a further 20 minutes or until the pastry is golden brown.

Using canned creamed rice

I have given the recipes for a whole can of creamed rice, but you could halve a can for 1 portion and store the remainder of the can in a cool place and use it on the next day. Naturally, the contents of the can may just be heated and served as an 'old-fashioned' rice pudding, but these recipes give a new touch to the homely rice pudding.

If you would rather make your own rice pudding then simmer 1½ oz. *round* (often called Carolina) rice with ¾ pint milk and sugar to taste until thick and creamy.

Apple rice bake

cooking time: 30 minutes
cooking appliance: oven

you will need for 2–3 servings:

1 can creamed rice   1 egg
1 can apple purée (use
   the tiny size sold for
   baby food)

1 Blend the ingredients together, put into an oven-proof dish.
2 Bake in the centre of a very moderate to moderate oven (350–375°F., Gas Mark 3–4) for approximately 30 minutes.
3 Serve with cream or ice cream.
To vary:
Use apricot or other fruit purée.

Rice soufflé

cooking time: 30 minutes
cooking appliance: oven

you will need for 2–3 servings:

2 eggs   1 oz. sugar
1 can creamed rice   flavouring (see below)

1 Separate the egg whites from the yolks – see below.
2 Blend the rice, egg yolks and sugar in a basin, add the flavouring.
3 Whisk the whites until very stiff; you should be able to turn the bowl upside down without the meringue mixture falling out. Use a proper egg whisk for this.
4 Fold the egg whites into the rice mixture.
5 Put into an oven-proof dish and bake for 30 minutes in the centre of a moderate oven (375°F., Gas Mark 4–5).
6 Serve at once.
To flavour
Chocolate: add 2 teaspoons cocoa powder or 1 tablespoon drinking chocolate powder.
Coffee: add 1–2 tablespoons instant coffee powder.
Lemon: add the finely grated rind of 1 or 2 lemons – NOT the juice.
Vanilla: add a few drops vanilla essence.
To separate egg yolks and whites
This is not easy to do at first.
The correct method is to crack the egg in the centre of the shell, then gently pull the two halves of the egg apart sufficiently for the egg white to drop out into a basin.
After this, pull the halves apart and put the egg yolk into another basin.
To make quite certain you get as much egg white as possible you can let the majority of the white fall into a basin, as described above, then tip the one half of the egg shell upside

down and let every drop of egg white come out. Next, tip the yolk out of the second half of the shell and hold this second half over the basin until there is no white left.

Perhaps the easiest way of all to separate egg white and egg yolk is to break the shell and pour the *whole* egg on to a saucer, put an egg cup over the yolk and pour the white into a basin.

Rose hip and rice soufflé

Use the recipe above, but omit the sugar and sweeten and flavour with 2 tablespoons of rose hip syrup. Cooking the syrup destroys the important Vitamin C content, so another method of introducing this is to make a sauce by heating 3–4 tablespoons of rose hip syrup with the juice of ½ lemon – DO NOT LET THE SYRUP BOIL. Serve hot sauce with the plain soufflé. If preferred, leave sauce unheated.

Caramelled rice

cooking time : 6 – 7 minutes
cooking appliances : boiling ring and
grill

you will need for 2–3 servings :

1 can creamed rice   2 oz. brown sugar
1 oz. flaked almonds

1 Heat the creamed rice for a few minutes.
2 Pour into a heat resistant servings dish.
3 Top with the almonds and brown sugar.
4 Brown under the grill.

Sweet omelettes

These make excellent desserts and incorporate important protein into your meal.

The instructions for making soufflé omelettes are on page 24 and although one *can* have a plain sweet omelette – see page 24 adding a little sugar to the beaten eggs, in place of seasoning, a soufflé omelette *looks* more interesting.

Orange omelette

cooking time : few minutes
cooking appliances : boiling ring and
grill – but see method

you will need for 2 servings :

3 eggs   1 large orange
½–1 oz. sugar   1 tablespoon cream
(depending on   from the top of the
personal taste)   milk

to cook :   **to decorate :**

1 oz. butter   sprinkling castor or
                               icing sugar

1 Separate the egg yolks from the whites.
2 Beat the egg yolks, sugar, the grated orange rind and cream together.
3 Whisk the egg whites until very stiff, fold into the yolk mixture.
4 Heat the butter and cook the omelette. As described on page 24 it is better to cook firstly over the heat of the boiling ring and then under the grill.
   If you have no grill however then cook *steadily* until just set on the boiling ring.
5 Cut the orange pulp into neat pieces.
6 Fill the omelette with this, fold and top with a little sugar.
7 Serve at once.
   This is only one of many flavourings. Here are others to try. Quantities are given for 3 eggs which is enough for 2 portions.
   Fruit omelette: omit orange rind and fill with canned apple purée, apricot purée or canned fruit. This is an excellent way of using up left-over canned fruit – this may be heated if wished, but the contrast between *cold* fruit and hot omelette is very delicious.
   Ice cream omelette: fill the omelette with ice cream and a little jam or redcurrant jelly.
   Jam or jelly omelette: one of the best known of French desserts is a soufflé omelette filled with very hot jam or redcurrant jelly. Fold the omelette and top with a little more jam or jelly.
   Nut omelette: add 1–2 oz. flaked almonds to the eggs. When the omelette is cooked and folded, sprinkle more nuts on top and brown under the grill for 1 minute, if possible.
   See page 25 for savoury omelette ideas.

Egg custards

An egg custard is a rather slow pudding to cook, but it is very easy.

Baked custard

cooking time : 1 hour
cooking appliance : oven

you will need for 1–2 servings :

1 egg   ½ pint milk
½–1 oz.
  sugar

1 Beat the egg and sugar thoroughly. This breaks up every particle of egg yolk and so you need not strain the custard.
2 Add the milk. If wished this can be heated but it is not essential.
3 Pour into pie dish or other oven-proof dish. To prevent curdling and drying round the edges it is a good idea to stand the dish of custard in a meat tin or dish of cold water.
Note: an even better safeguard is to bake the custard for 20–30 minutes of the cooking time, until the mixture is just getting hot, then stand this in a dish of *warm* water.
4 Bake for about 1 hour, until set, in a slow oven (275–300°F., Gas Mark 1–2).

To vary :
Spiced custard: add a little mixed spice or grated nutmeg to the eggs and sugar and top the custard with spice or nutmeg before baking.
Chocolate custard: blend 1–2 teaspoons cocoa powder or 1 tablespoon drinking chocolate powder with the egg yolks and sugar.
Bread and butter pudding: cut a slice of bread and butter. Divide into triangles. Put into the dish with 1 oz. dried fruit. Add the custard and a sprinkling of sugar, and cook as above.
Swiss roll pudding: put 2 thin slices of Swiss roll in the dish. Add the custard and a sprinkling of sugar, cook as above.

'Boiled'* custard

cooking time : 20 minutes
cooking appliance : boiling ring

you will need for 1–2 servings :

1 egg   ½ pint milk
½–1 oz. sugar

1 The method of making is as baked custard.
2 Pour into the top of a double saucepan and stand over the bottom of the double saucepan filled with *hot* NOT boiling water and cook, stirring from time to time, until thickened; *or* keep in the basin and stand this over the hot water.

* This is, of course, a wrong name to give a custard, for if you *did* boil the egg and milk the mixture would curdle.

To vary :
Crumb custard: make the custard and when nearly set, add 1 crumbled macaroon biscuit and 1 oz. flaked almonds. Serve in 2 glasses topped with glacé cherries.

Floating islands

This is a classic French pudding based on an egg custard and it makes a delicious hot or cold dessert – the latter is the more usual.

cooking time: 25 minutes
cooking appliance: boiling ring

you will need for 2–3 servings :

2 eggs   ¾ pint milk
3 oz. sugar   few drops vanilla essence

1 Separate the egg yolks from the whites.
2 Whisk the egg whites until they are very stiff then fold in 2 oz. of sugar.
3 Put the milk and the vanilla essence into a frying pan and heat.
4 Drop spoonfuls of the meringue mixture on to the hot but NOT boiling milk.
5 Poach on one side for about 1½ minutes then turn and poach on the second side.
6 Lift off with a fish slice and cool on a sieve or plate.
7 Meanwhile, beat the egg yolks and rest of sugar and strain the milk over the yolk mixture.
8 Cook as boiled custard and when thickened top with the meringue.

To vary :
Pour a little rose hip syrup or cherry brandy over the meringue balls just before serving.

This is delicious served with very hot, canned black cherries.

Some hot puddings with fruit

Baked apples

Buy large cooking apples and core them (with

a sharp knife or apple corer). Split the skin round the centre – so this does not break badly during cooking.

Stand in a dish and cook for about 1 hour in the centre of a moderate to moderately hot oven (375–400°F., Gas Mark 5–6).

The apple centre can be filled with:

a golden syrup or honey.

b a tiny knob of butter and sugar (preferably brown).

c dried fruit or jam.

If you have no oven you can cook the apple in a deep soup plate over a saucepan of boiling water. Cover the plate with foil or a saucepan lid. The apples take about 45 minutes to cook.

Bananas in orange sauce

Heat ½ oz. butter in a frying pan with 1 oz. sugar. Add the juice of 1 orange and then put 1 large banana into the sauce and cook for 5–6 minutes. Turn during cooking.

For special occasions, flavour the sauce with brandy or rum.

Peaches

Halved fresh peaches may be cooked in the same way or heat canned peaches in the syrup.

Pears

These can be cooked in the same kind of syrup or simmered in sweetened red wine.

Peel, halve and core a *firm* dessert pear.

Heat ¼ pint red wine with 1 oz. sugar and simmer the pear in this for 10 minutes until pale pink in colour. Serve very hot with cream.

Pineapple rings

They are very good heated in a sauce, as banana, but perhaps the best hot pudding is a fritter – see below.

Pineapple fritters

cooking time: 6 – 7 minutes
cooking appliance: boiling ring

you will need for 2 servings:

4 rings canned pineapple   ½ oz. flour

for the batter:

2 oz. self-raising flour   ¼ pint milk
1 egg

to fry: **to coat:**

2 oz. fat   1 oz. sugar

1 Drain pineapple rings well. Sprinkle with the flour, it does not matter if plain or self-raising flour is used.

2 Make a smooth batter by beating the flour with the egg and milk.

3 Dip the rings of pineapple in this then fry on either side in the hot fat.

4 Drain on kitchen roll and sprinkle with sugar.

To vary:

With apple: thin rings of raw apple may be coated and fried in the same way.

With banana: halved bananas may be coated and fried in the same way.

Zabaione

This is one of the most famous of Italian desserts and is often called Zabaglione. It is delicious for a special dessert and yet quick to prepare. Zabaione is ideal for anyone on a light diet when the appetite needs tempting.

cooking time: few minutes
cooking appliance: boiling ring

you will need for 2–3 servings:

3 egg yolks   2–3 tablespoons
2–3 oz. sugar   Marsala*

*This is correct but sweet sherry could be used.

1 Put egg yolks and sugar into a basin, whisk hard for 1 minute.

2 Stand over a saucepan of hot water and whisk until light and frothy.

3 Add the wine and continue whisking until the mixture is very light and thickened.

4 Serve as soon as this is made.

To vary:

It is excellent by itself or served over hot, canned black cherries or cold, fresh or frozen raspberries.

Cakes

Cakes that need cooking

There are so many cookery books that specialise in cake recipes baked in the oven that I am just giving several recipes that are made *without* an oven; so you can enjoy a home-made cake on occasions.

Steamed fruit cake

cooking time: $1\frac{1}{2}$ hours
cooking appliance: boiling ring

you will need for 8–10 servings:

6 oz. self-raising flour	3 oz. margarine or butter
4 oz. sugar	3 tablespoons milk
6 oz. mixed dried fruit	2 eggs

Grease a 6 inch cake tin thoroughly. DO NOT use one with a loose base.
Mix the flour, sugar and fruit.
Heat the margarine or butter and milk until the fat melts, cool then beat into the flour mixture. Lastly add the eggs and beat well. Put the mixture into the tin. Cover with greased, greaseproof paper and put into a steamer over boiling water and cook for $1\frac{1}{2}$ hours. Turn out when cooked.
Naturally this cake is not crisp; when cooked, if you have a grill, you could brown and crisp the top with the heat turned down very low.
To vary:
With mixed spice: add 1 level teaspoon mixed spice to the flour.
With marmalade: omit 2 tablespoons milk and add 1 good tablespoon of orange marmalade.

Welsh cakes

cooking time: 8 – 10 minutes
cooking appliance: boiling ring

you will need for 4–5 servings:

4 oz. self-raising flour	2 oz. dried fruit
2 oz. margarine or butter	little milk
2 oz. sugar	

to cook:

$\frac{1}{2}$ oz. fat

1 Put the flour into a mixing bowl.
2 Rub in the fat until like fine breadcrumbs, add the sugar and fruit.
3 Stir in barely 1 tablespoon milk. The mixture must be sufficiently firm to press or roll out.
4 Sprinkle a very little flour on the working surface; press out the dough with a floured hand into a neat circle just over $\frac{1}{4}$ inch thick or roll out if preferred. If you have no rolling pin use an empty milk bottle.
5 Cut into 4–5 portions.
6 Rub the frying pan with the fat and heat slowly.
7 Put in the cakes. Cook on either side for 2 minutes until brown. Then turn the heat very low so they cook more slowly.
The cakes are cooked when they feel firm to the touch.
Note:
They are best if eaten fresh.

Quick doughnuts

cooking time: 7 – 8 minutes
cooking appliance: boiling ring

you will need for 4 servings:

4 oz. self-raising flour	1 egg
1 oz. margarine	1 tablespoon milk
1 oz. sugar	

to fry:	**to coat:**
2 oz. fat	1 oz. sugar

1 Put the flour into a basin.
2 Rub in the margarine, add the sugar, the egg and milk. Beat well together.
3 Heat the fat in a pan.
4 Put in spoonfuls of the mixture, fry on one side fairly quickly, turn and fry on the second side, then lower the heat and cook until firm to the touch.
5 Take out of the pan, drain on kitchen paper, then roll in sugar.

Cakes that need no cooking

There are many cakes you can buy today which keep very well in carefully packed containers; but here are a few recipes you can make without any cooking at all.

Coconut fingers

no cooking

you will need for 4–6 servings :

4 tablespoons sweetened condensed milk
5 oz. desiccated coconut

a little rice paper*

*Obtainable in packets from stationers.

1 Mix condensed milk and coconut together.
2 Spread over the rice paper and leave overnight to harden.
3 Cut into fingers with a sharp knife dipped into hot water.
To vary :
Form the mixture into pyramid shapes with damp fingers. Put on the rice paper and leave to set. Tear or cut round the paper to give a neat shape.
Chocolate coconut fingers: melt 2 oz. plain chocolate in a basin over hot water and spread the chocolate over the fingers with a knife dipped in hot water.
Fruity coconut fingers: mix 1 oz. sultanas and 1 oz. chopped glacé cherries with the condensed milk and coconut.

Chocolate party gâteau

no cooking

you will need for 6–8 servings :

8 oz. plain chocolate
1 *level* tablespoon golden syrup or honey
2 eggs

1 oz. flaked almonds
8 oz. plain biscuits (digestive) or semi-sweet biscuits

to decorate :

¼ pint thick cream

1 oz. flaked almonds

1 Break the chocolate into pieces and put into a basin over hot NOT boiling water, add the golden syrup and allow to melt.

2 Add the eggs and beat well over the hot water until a smooth, thick, light mixture; an egg whisk is ideal for this.
3 Cool slightly then add the almonds and the biscuits, broken into small pieces.
4 Put into a 5–6 inch, buttered cake tin. Allow to set then turn out.
5 Either serve plain or for special occasions top with the whipped cream and nuts.
To vary :
With coffee: add ½ tablespoon instant coffee at stage 1.

Chocolate clusters

no cooking

you will need for 8–9 servings :

4 oz. plain chocolate

2-3 oz. breakfast cereal

1 Melt the chocolate in a basin over hot water, cool slightly, stir in the breakfast cereal and coat thoroughly in the chocolate.
2 Put in small heaps on a flat plate or tin and allow to set.

Marshmallow pyramids

no cooking

you will need for 8–10 servings :

2 oz. marshmallows
2 oz. fudge (vanilla flavour)

½ oz. butter
2½ oz. cornflakes or other breakfast cereal

1 Heat the marshmallows, fudge and butter over a very low heat in the saucepan. Cool then add the cereal.
2 Stir well together then form into pyramid shapes on a flat plate or tin and leave to set.

Dishes to keep you fit

Most sensible people today are anxious to keep a slim figure and a well-planned diet is an essential towards either losing weight or maintaining a good weight. It is unwise to follow diets that do not include the important foods – proteins, fresh fruit, vegetables, etc., for you may become very slender at the risk of losing energy and health.

What are the golden rules of keeping slim?

To plan meals around the protein foods – eggs, cheese, meat, etc.

To 'fill up' with plenty of vegetables and salads and citrus fruits. Other fruits, such as apples and bananas may have to be restricted slightly if you wish to lose weight and so may vegetables that contain starch, e.g. peas, beans, potatoes.

To include small amounts only of the carbohydrate foods – starches and sugar.

To avoid 'nibbling' between meals.

Eating out

One of the problems of cooking for one or two people in a 'bedsitter', is that it is rather difficult to use up a wide variety of ingredients, therefore one tends to have simple and uncomplicated dishes. When you eat out therefore look for those more unusual foods that you would find difficult to cook.

Many people who are 'figure conscious' often say it is difficult to keep to a low calorie or health food type of diet when you have to eat in restaurants. Once upon a time this comment might have been true, but today there are many places which concentrate on excellent salads and foods with fresh vegetables.

Some of the dishes on the following pages are a speciality of a famous health food restaurant – and I have reproduced, with their kind permission, a selection of their recipes.

Soup gives one a feeling of warmth and well-being and is a wise choice when on a slimming diet, providing the soups contain low-calorie foods. Here are four interesting recipes; where milk is mentioned in the recipes you could use skimmed milk.

Carrot soup

cooking time : 30 minutes
cooking appliance : boiling ring

you will need for 2 servings :

1 oz. margarine	$\frac{1}{2}$ pint water
1 onion (or use dehydrated onion)	seasoning
	$\frac{1}{2}$ pint milk
8 oz. carrots	

to garnish :
chopped parsley

1 Heat the margarine in a saucepan and toss the grated onion and grated carrots in this for a few minutes.
2 Cover with the water, season and simmer for 20 minutes.
3 Beat hard and when smooth add the milk and heat, taste and re-season if wished. Top with the chopped parsley.
Note :
When not slimming, top with a little cream and parsley.

Cucumber soup

A similar soup is made using peeled, grated cucumber in place of carrot. This is delicious served cold.

French onion soup

To make this in the most simple way, you could use dehydrated onions and simmer them in stock until tender. The soup is then topped with grated cheese.
Note :
When not slimming, top with squares of bread and grated cheese and brown under the grill.

Fruit soups

Cherries make an excellent soup, but most sharp fruits make delicious soups, which are extremely popular on the Continent.
Simmer the fruit with enough water to make a thin purée, add a little lemon juice to give a sharp refreshing flavour. Either sweeten with sugar or sugar substitute but make sure the

soup is not too sweet as you need this to sharpen your appetite for the main course.

Mushroom pie

cooking time: 15 minutes
cooking appliances: boiling ring and
grill or oven

you will need for 2 servings:

1 oz. margarine or butter
1 oz. flour or ½ oz. cornflour
¼ pint water
½ teaspoon yeast extract
6 oz. button mushrooms

for the topping:
creamed potato

to garnish:
sliced tomato
chopped parsley

1 Heat the margarine or butter, then stir in the flour and cook for 2–3 minutes.
2 Gradually blend in the water, add the yeast extract and bring to the boil for 2–3 minutes, stirring well. Cook until a smooth sauce.
3 Wash, dry and quarter the mushrooms, add to the sauce and simmer for 3–4 minutes, stir well.
4 Put into one dish or 2 individual dishes, top with piped potato (or just pile the potato on top).
5 Brown under the grill.
6 Garnish with sliced tomato and chopped parsley.
Note:
If preferred, brown in a moderately hot oven. This recipe is not particularly low calorie as it includes flour and potatoes – the mushrooms could be simmered in an unthickened stock if wished and the amount of potato used can be very little.

Vegetable hot pot

A small quantity of potato is often included in some diets and this recipe makes a good meal of vegetables and cheese.

cooking time: 2 hours 10 minutes
cooking appliances: boiling ring and
oven

you will need for 2–3 servings:

3 medium potatoes
seasoning
1 oz. margarine
2 medium onions
2 medium carrots
3 sticks celery
8 oz. peas
3–4 oz. mushrooms
¼ pint water
1 teaspoon yeast extract

for the topping:
3–4 oz. grated cheese

1 Peel and slice the potatoes and cook in well seasoned water for 5 minutes, then strain.
2 Put half the potatoes at the bottom of the casserole.
3 Heat the margarine and toss the peeled, sliced onions in this.
4 Slice the carrots thinly, chop the celery and put them all, with the peas and mushrooms, in the dish, ending with the remainder of the potatoes.
5 Blend the water and yeast extract, pour over the vegetables (add extra seasoning if wished).
6 Bake for 1¼ hours in the centre of a very moderate to moderate oven (350–375°F., Gas Mark 3–4), remove from the oven, top with the cheese and return to the oven for a further 45 minutes.
To vary:
If you have no oven, cook all the vegetables in a saucepan in the yeast flavoured liquid. When tender (they will take about 1 hour), put into a dish and top with cheese.

Egg with yoghourt and tomato purée

cooking time: 10 minutes
cooking appliance: boiling ring

you will need for 2 servings:

4 eggs
5 oz. carton natural yoghourt
1–2 teaspoons tomato purée
seasoning

to garnish:
paprika pepper

1 Hard-boil the eggs, shell and cool.
2 Blend the yoghourt with the purée and season well.
3 Coat the eggs with this and top with paprika. This can be served by itself or as part of a salad.

To vary:

To give a more piquant dressing, a little oil and vinegar or oil and lemon juice may be added.

Stuffed peppers

cooking time: 30 minutes approx.
cooking appliances: boiling ring and
                  oven

you will need for 2 servings:

2 green peppers	2 oz. cooked rice or
½ oz. margarine	sweet corn
2 onions	3 oz. nutmeat*
2 tomatoes	seasoning
2 oz. cheese	pinch powdered sage
1 tablespoon flageolet	and thyme
(optional)	1–2 tablespoons
	tomato ketchup

to serve:

plain boiled or saffron
    rice (see page 77)

* Nutmeat can be bought from health food stores.

1 Cut the peppers in halves crossways. Take out the centres and seeds.
2 Put into boiling, salted water and cook very gently for 5 minutes. Drain well.
3 Heat the margarine and brown the chopped onions slightly.
4 Add the chopped, skinned tomatoes, grated cheese, flageolet and cooked rice or sweet corn.
5 Make up the nutmeat with boiling water (as instructions on the nutmeat packet) and add to the rest of the ingredients.
6 Season with salt and pepper and the powdered sage and thyme.
7 To moisten, add the tomato ketchup.
8 Pile into the halved peppers.
9 Place the stuffed peppers in a greased baking tin or oven-proof dish, cover with aluminium foil and bake for approximately 20 minutes in a moderately hot oven.
10 Serve with plain boiled or saffron rice.

Apple meringue

cooking time: about 20 minutes

cooking appliances: boiling ring and
                  oven

you will need for 2 servings:

2 large cooking apples	**for the topping:**
1 tablespoon water	
granulated sugar	1 egg white
1 egg yolk	2 oz. castor sugar

1 Peel and core apples. Cut into thin slices and put into a saucepan with the water. Cover and simmer gently until apples are reduced to a purée. Sweeten to taste with granulated sugar and beat in egg yolk. Turn into two individual ovenproof dishes.
2 Whisk egg white until stiff and peaky. Gradually beat in half the castor sugar, a teaspoon at a time, and fold in the remainder. Pipe in swirls or spoon on top of the apple.
3 Bake the meringue for about 3 minutes in a hot oven, (425–450°F., Gas Mark 6–7) until golden brown, or put for a few minutes under the grill to brown.

Note:

If on a strict diet, omit the meringue and sweeten the apples with liquid sweetener. Canned apple purée can also be used.

Fresh fruit salad

you will need for 2 servings:

8 oz. strawberries	1 banana
4 oz. grapes	juice of ½ small lemon
4 oz. cherries	3 tablespoons castor
1 orange	sugar
1 dessert apple	1 tablespoon cider or
	sherry (optional)

1 Hull and halve strawberries.
2 Wash grapes and cherries, if desired you may halve and remove the pips and stones.
3 Peel orange, divide into segments and carefully remove pith and membrane.
4 Peel, core and slice apple.
5 Peel and slice banana and sprinkle both the apple and banana with lemon juice, this prevents discolouration.
6 Arrange the fruit in a fruit bowl.
7 Sift sugar over the fruit and pour over the cider or sherry, if desired.
8 Allow to stand for about 30 minutes in a cool place, to marinate and for the syrup to form.

Easy salads for slimming

Blend the ingredients together. Naturally you will avoid mayonnaise when on a diet, so toss in lemon juice unless a special dressing is given. Here are some of the interesting flavours to try:

Grated or shredded cooked beetroot, peeled, chopped dessert apple, chopped celery and finely chopped spring onions.

Grated or shredded cooked beetroot and sprigs of watercress. This is excellent if mixed with natural yoghourt.

Thinly sliced cucumber and diced, ripe melon. Toss in natural yoghourt.

Slice well-washed button mushrooms (raw mushrooms are excellent in all salads if they are small and tender); blend with sliced green pepper, a few peanuts or cashew nuts and raisins. Be sparing with the raisins on a diet.

Blend a small quantity of well-drained, finely chopped, canned pineapple with shredded cabbage, halved black grapes (with the seeds removed), shredded green pepper, chopped parsley. Add a few peanuts for a light meal.

Segments of fresh orange and chopped chicory.

Thin strips of green pepper, raisins and chopped walnuts or whole cashew nuts make another interesting salad, but avoid too many raisins if you are on a strict diet.

Blend sliced tomato and bean shoots, fresh or canned; this is an excellent way to use up left-over canned bean shoots if you have used some in cooking, see page 56.

Shred a very little raw spinach finely, blend with finely chopped onion and top with chopped hard-boiled egg. This salad is very good for you, and very excellent when the spinach is really fresh. Toss in plenty of well seasoned lemon juice or use a little cider vinegar if wished.

Dishes for special diets

The recipes in this book have been planned to provide nutritious and interesting dishes, with no particular diet in mind.

You will however find many recipes that are suitable for rather special diets. If you wish to put on weight, DO NOT eat only the carbohydrate foods. You can include more of these in comparison with people who wish to *lose* weight but have plenty of protein foods as well; also salads and vegetables.

Drink milk or milky beverages (cocoa, chocolate, malted milk) at night time and midmorning.

Cook meat etc., in milk sauces, such as the fricassée.

Fricassée of chicken

cooking time: 15 – 20 minutes
cooking appliance: boiling ring

you will need for 1 serving:

1 joint frying chicken
small quantity onion
(or onion soup
powder)
¼ pint water
seasoning

¼ pint milk or use
half milk and half
thin cream
1½ level teaspoons
cornflour
½ oz. butter

1 Allow the chicken to defrost if it has been frozen, divide into 2 pieces and put into a saucepan.
2 Add the onion and water and seasoning or about 2–3 teaspoons dehydrated onion soup powder blended with the water and little, if any, seasoning and pour this over the chicken.
3 Simmer for 10 minutes.
4 Blend the milk or milk and cream and cornflour smoothly together. Add to the liquid in the pan, stir well as you do so and add the butter.
5 Allow the mixture to simmer gently until the chicken is tender.

To vary :

Use very tender fillet of veal or diced lean lamb.

Add frozen peas at stage 4 or sliced mushrooms. These are inclined to spoil the colour of the sauce, so could be fried separately and stirred into the sauce at the last minute.

Try to relax and enjoy your meals, as this is one reason why you may be under-weight.

If you have a gastric disorder or some kind of stomach ulcer

Often this is due to stress and strain so you too should try to relax, and put any worries behind you at meal time and when you go to bed.

Never go longer than 2 hours without having something to eat – it could be just biscuit and milk or a light meal.

Have smaller meals more often than before you had gastric trouble; you may find this is all you need to do to cure the complaint.

Avoid fatty, fried, highly spiced foods or indigestible ingredients, e.g. onion, cooked cheese.

The fricassée above would be splendid for you but either omit the onion altogether or just put an onion into the liquid to give flavour and take it out.

Eggs, white fish, chicken, sweetbreads, tripe, are all the kind of protein foods to choose while you are unwell.

To cook tripe

Buy 8 oz. 'dressed' tripe. Cut into small pieces, blanch this as page 62 then cook as the chicken fricassée.

Index

ANCHOVY:
Anchovy sauce, 74
Anchovy tomato bake, 34
And potato au gratin, 34
APPLE:
And cream cheese, 78
And ice cream whip, 79
Apple fritters, 86
Apple meringue, 91
Apple rice bake, 83
Baked, 85
ARTICHOKE, Globe:
Fresh, to prepare/cook, 64
New ways to serve, 64
Other ways to buy, 64
ARTICHOKE, Jerusalem:
Fresh, to prepare/cook, 64
Artichoke hors d'oeuvre, 15
ASPARAGUS:
Fresh, to prepare/cook, 64
New ways to serve, 64
Other ways to buy, 64
A la Polonaise, 15
And ham chowder, 20
And ham rolls, 15
And tuna chowder, 20
Asparagus cheese, 25
Asparagus soufflé, 25
With cheese 14
With cream cheese, 14
AUBERGINE:
Fresh, to prepare, 64
Fried, 64
Stuffed, 64
AVOCADO PEARS:
And cream cheese salad, 72
Canapés, 17
With vinaigrette dressing, 16
Curried, and prawns, 17

BACON:
Cuts of, pre-packed, 50
Fried, 55
Gammon, boiled, 53
Grilled, 55
And cheese custard, 28

And cod, 36
With potato/onion, 36
With tomato, 36
And potato chowder, 19
And tomato chowder, 18
Bacon omelette, 25
Fried bacon with apple, 55
With canned fruit, 55
With egg, 55
Baked bloater, 35
With onions, tomato, 35
With tomatoes, etc., 35
Baked buckling, 35
With onions, tomato, 35
With tomatoes, etc., 35
Baked cheese, 28
With egg, 28
With potato, 28
With tomato, 28
Baked cod, 36
Baked cod in milk, 36
With cream, 36
With lemon, 36
With mayonnaise, 36
With parsley, 36
Baked cod in wine/cider, 38
Baked custard, 85
Baked eggs, 21
Baked herrings, 43
With apple, 43
With dates, 43
With fish paste, 43
With prawns or shrimps, 43
With prunes, 43
BANANA:
Banana fritters, 86
Banana split, 79
In orange sauce, 86
Lemon banana, 79
Barbecue sauce, 61
Barbecued eggs, 22
Barbecued ham, 60
Barbecued luncheon meat, 61
BEANS:
Bean shoots, 66
Broad beans, 65

Green beans, 65
New ways to serve, 65
Other ways to buy, 65
Haricot, butter beans, 65
Bean, bacon bake, 65
Bean, cheese baké, 65
Bean, cheese casserole, 65
Bean, ham, egg bake, 65
Bean salad, 71
BEEF:
Cuts of, to choose, 49
And mushroom soup, 19
BEETROOT:
When fresh, 66
Fresh, to prepare/cook, 66
New ways to serve, 66
Other ways to buy, 66
Beetroot, apple salad, 71
Borsch, 20
BLOATER:
Baked with tomatoes, etc., 35
Fried, 35
Grilled, lemon flavour, 35
Grilled, tomato coating, 35
Boiled custard, 85
Boiled eggs, 21
Borsch, 20
Bread/butter pudding, 85
Bread omelette, 25
BROCCOLI:
To prepare/cook, 66
Brown sauce, 67
Browned eggs, 23
BRUSSELS SPROUTS:
Fresh, to prepare/cook, 66
New ways to serve, 66
Other ways to buy, 66
BUCKLING:
Baked, onion/tomatoes, 35
Baked, tomatoes, etc., 35
Fried, 35
Grilled, lemon flavour, 35
Grilled, tomato coating, 35
Savoury buckling salad, 36
Burgundy stew: variations, 58

CABBAGE:
Fresh, to prepare/cook, 67
New way to serve, 67
CAKES:
Chocolate clusters, 88
Chocolate party gâteau, 88
With coffee, 88
Coconut fingers, 88
Chocolate 88
Fruity, 88
Marshmallow pyramids, 88
Quick doughnuts, 87
Steamed fruit cake, 87
With marmalade, 87
With mixed spice, 87
Welsh cakes, 87
Caramel oranges, 79
Caramelled rice, 84
CARROT:
Fresh, to prepare/cook, 67
New ways to serve, 67
Other ways to buy, 67
Carrot salad, 71
Carrot soup, 19
Carrot soup, slimming, 89
CASSEROLED DISHES AND
STEWS:
Bean/cheese casserole, 65
Burgundy stew: variations, 58
Curried meat/chicken No. 1, 57
Variations, 57
Curried meat/chicken No. 2, 58
Curried eggs, 58
Curried fish, 58
Fish casseroles, 40
Fish and mushroom, 40
Fish and tomato, 40
Fish, tomato/onion, 40
Pot roast, 59
To make gravy, 59
Variations, 59
Stew Americaine, 57
With corned beef, 57
With kidneys, 57
With mixed vegetables, 57

CAULIFLOWER:
Fresh, to prepare/cook, 67
New ways to serve, 67
Other ways to buy, 67
Caviare, 32
CELERIAC:
To prepare/cook, 67
CELERY:
To use celery, 67
Celery/cheese toast, 28
CHEESE:
Buying, storing, grating, 26, 27
Hard/soft, 26
Bacon, cheese custard, 28
Baked cheese, 28
With egg, 28
With potato, 28
With tomato, 28
Celery, cheese toast, 28
Cheese custard, 28
Cheese fingers, 27
Cheese omelette, 25
Cheese potatoes, 70
Cheese salads
Egg and cheese, 27
Scrambled cheese, 27
Cheese sauce, 74
Cheese soufflé, 26
Cheese, vegetable bake, 28
Fish, cheese custard, 28
Fried cheese, 28
Ham, cheese toast, 28
Open sandwiches, 27
Sardine, cheese toast, 28
Toasted cheese, 28
Vegetable, cheese custard, 28
With fish, 27
With fruit, 27
With meat, 27
With vegetables, 27
CHICKEN:
For frying/grilling, 56
To fry, 56
Chicken chop suey, 56
Fricassée of, 92
Fried: with bananas, 56
With creamed corn, 56
With vegetables, 56
With walnuts 56
Grilled: variations, 56, 57
CHICORY:
To cook/serve, 67
Chocolate clusters, 88
Chocolate custard 85
Chocolate party gâteau, 88
Coconut fingers, 88
Chocolate, 88
Fruity, 88
COD:
Bacon and cod, 36
With potato or onion, 36
With tomato, 36
Baked, 36
Baked cod in milk, 36
With cream, 36
With lemon, 36
With mayonnaise, 36
With parsley, 36
Baked cod with wine/cider, 38
Cod in cider, 38
And vegetable medley, 38
Cod in cider sauce, 38
Cod in lemon butter, 37
Cod in orange butter, 37
Cod in savoury butter, 37
Curried, 37
Fried, 36
With cucumber, 37
With cucumber, ham, 37
Grilled cod with bacon, 37
With cheese, 37
With lemon, 37
With mustard, 37
Poached, 38
Coleslaw, 71

Consommé plus, 20
CORN ON THE COB:
Fresh, to prepare/cook, 68
New ways to serve, 68
Other ways to buy, 68
Corn, chicken soup, 20
Corn tomato soup, 20
COURGETTES:
Fresh, to prepare/cook, 68
New ways to serve, 68
CRAB:
Fresh, to prepare, 39
Crab salad, 39
Curried, 39
Devilled, 39
Cream of mushroom soup, 19
Cream of vegetable soup, 20
Creamed cod roe, 38
Crumb custard, 85
CUCUMBER:
To use cucumber, 68
Cucumber soup, 89
Curried avocado, prawns, 17
Curried cod, 37
Curried crab, 85
Curried eggs, 22
Curried fish, 58
Curried lobster, 40
Curried meat/chicken, 57, 58
Curried soup, 20
Curried steak, 54
Curried stewing steak, 60
Curries, to serve with, 58
Curry sauce, 58
CUSTARD:
Bacon, cheese, 28
Baked, 85
'Boiled', 85
Cheese, 28
Chocolate, 85
Crumb, 85
Fish, cheese, 28
Spiced, 85
Vegetable, cheese, 28

DESSERTS, cold:
Apple, cream cheese, 78
Apple and ice cream, 79
Banana split, 79
Caramel oranges, 79
Cherry milk jelly, 81
Cream jelly, 81
Evaporated milk jelly, 81
Fruit cocktails, 12
Fruit filled jellies, 81
Fruit salad, fresh, 91
Ice cream, 82
With fruit, 82
With nuts and chocolate, 82
With redcurrant jelly, 82
Lemon bananas, 79
Melon, 80
Sherry melon, 80
With raspberry sauce, 80
Milk jelly, 81
Pineapple, 80
Sponge flan, 81
Strawberries, 80
Yoghourt, 82
Devilled crab, 39
Devilled eggs, 23
Devilled lobster, 39
Devilled lobster, 39
Doughnuts, quick, 87

Eel, smoked, 13
EGGS, see also OMELETTES
and SOUFFLÉS:
To separate, 83
Baked, 21
Barbecued, 22
Boiled, 21
Browned, 23
Curried, 22
Devilled, 23
Egg, anchovy salad, 17

Egg and cheese, 21
Egg, cheese salad, 27
Egg Florentine, 22
Egg mayonnaise, 17
Egg Mornay, 22
Egg, prawn mayonnaise, 17
Egg salad, 71
Egg, sardine mayonnaise, 17
Egg sauce, 74
Egg, tomato cheese sauce, 22
Egg with vegetables, 21
Egg with yoghourt, etc., 90
Fried, 23
Hard-boiled, 22
Poached, 23
Poached egg on haddock, 23
Savoury poached, 23
Scrambled, 24
Soft-boiled, 21
Swiss eggs, 21
Tuna eggs, 23
Endive, 68
Evaporated milk cheese sauce, 74

Fat, disposal of, 56
FISH:
To buy fresh: 29
Freshwater fish, 32
Freshwater fish, frozen, 32
Oily fish, 31
Oily fish, canned, 31
Oily fish, frozen, 31
Roes, 32
Roes, canned, 32
Shellfish, 30
Shellfish, canned, 31
Shellfish, frozen, 30
Smoked fish, 30
Smoked fish, frozen, 30
White fish, 29
White fish, frozen, 29
Cooking fish
Baking, boiling, frying, 32, 33
Grilling, poaching, roasting,
32, 33
'oven-frying', steaming, 33, 34
Fish in a casserole, 33
Egg and crumb coating, 33
Fish dishes, see also ANCHOVY,
BLOATER, BUCKLING,
COD, ETC.
Flavourings for, 34
(Capers, fish pastes, gherkins
herbs, lemon, mayonnaise,
tomato)
Curried fish, 58
Fish, cheese custard, 28
Fish cakes, 40
Salmon fish cakes, 46
Fish casseroles, 40
Mushroom, 40
Tomato, 40
Tomato and onion, 40
Fish fingers, 41
Fish soup, 18
FLAN sponge: fillings, 81
Chocolate/coffee, 81
Chocolate/pear, 82
Ice cream/fruit, 82
Floating islands, 85
Foil cooked chops, 63
Steak, 62
FRANKFURTERS:
To cook, 59
With mustard tomato sauce, 59
French onion soup, 89
Fricassée of chicken, 92
Variations, 93
Fried aubergine, 64
Fried bloaters, 35
Fried buckling, 35
Fried cheese, 28
Fried chicken, banana, 56
With creamed corn, 56
With vegetables, 56
With walnuts, 56

Fried cod, 36
With cucumber, ham, 37
Fried cod's roe, 38
Fried eggs, 23
Fried halibut, 42
Fried herring, 43
Fried herring roes, 44
Fried scallops, 47
Fried sweetbreads, 62
Fruit cake, steamed, 87
Variations, 87
Fruit cocktails, 12
Fruit omelette, 84
Fruit pies, 82
Fruit salad, fresh, 91
Fruit soup, 89
Fruit supreme, 12
Fruity coconut fingers, 88
GAMMON:
To boil, 53
Garlic, 68
Goulash, 60
GRAPEFRUIT:
To grill, 12
With fruit juice 12
With honey, etc., 12
With sherry, 12
Grilled bloater, lemon flavour, 35
With tomato coating, 35
Grilled buckling, lemon flavour, 35
With tomato coating, 35
Grilled cod, with bacon, 37
With cheese, 37
With lemon, 37
With mustard, 37
Grilled cod's roe, 39
With cheese, 39
Grilled herrings 43

HADDOCK:
Smoked, with mushrooms, 42
With tomatoes, 42
Steamed haddock, 41
With mayonnaise, 41
With mushrooms, 41
With paprika, 41
With tomato juice, 41
Stuffed 41
HALIBUT:
Fried, 42
In brown butter 42
In tomato cucumber sauce, 42
In yoghourt, 42
Parmesan halibut, 42
Roasted halibut, 42
HAM, canned or cooked, 60
Barbecued, 60
Ham and cheese toast, 28
Ham omelette, 25
Pineapple roast, 60
HAMBURGERS, frozen, 59
With cheese, 59
With curry sauce, 60
With pineapple, 59
Hard-boiled eggs, 22
Hasty cassoulet, 60
Herb omelette, 25
HERRING:
To remove backbone, 42
Baked, 43
With apple, 43
With dates, 43
With fish paste, 43
With prawns or shrimps, 43
With prunes, 43
Fried, 43
Grilled, 43
Herring and lemon, 43
Herring salad, 44
With beetroot, 44
With corn, 44
With egg, 44
With lemon/vinegar, 44
Herring, tomatoes, etc., 43
Savoury grilled, 43
Stuffed fried, 43

HORS D'OEUVRE:
Artichoke, 15
Asparagus, 14
 A la Polonaise, 15
 And ham rolls, 15
 With cheese, 14
 With cream cheese, 14
Avocado canapés, 17
Avocado pear, 16
 Curried with prawns, 17
 With vinaigrette, 16
Chopped liver, 18
Egg, anchovy salad, 17
Egg, prawn mayonnaise, 17
Egg, sardine mayonnaise, 17
Egg mayonnaise, 17
Fish, 13
Fruit cocktails, 12
Fruit supreme, 12
Grilled grapefruit, 12
Meat, 14
 Pâté, 14
 Salami, 14
Melon, 13
Mixed hors d'oeuvre. 14
Smoked eel, 13
Smoked mackerel, 13
Smoked salmon, 14
Smoked trout, 13
Soufflé tomatoes, 15
Stuffed tomatoes, 15, 16
Tomato salad, 13

ICE CREAM:
To serve, 82
Ice cream omelette, 84
With fruit, 82
With nuts and chocolate, 82
With redcurrant jelly, 82

Jam omelette, 84
JELLY:
To use packet jelly, 81
Cherry milk, 81
Cream, 81
Evaporated milk, 81
Fruit filled, 81
Jelly omelette, 84
Milk, 81

Kedgeree No. 1, No. 2, 77
KIDNEYS:
Canned: Variations, 60
Fresh, to cook, 60
Kippers, 44

LAMB OR MUTTON:
Cuts of, to choose, 50
Fried chops with cream, 55
 With pineapple, 56
 With prunes, 56
 With savoury sauce, 56
 With soup, 56
 With tomato purée, 56
Grilled chops, 56
 Wth orange, 56
 With spaghetti and
  mushrooms, 56
LEEK:
Fresh, to prepare/cook, 68
New ways to serve, 68
Lemon banana, 79
Lemon sole mornay, 48
LETTUCE:
To prepare/store, 68
LIVER:
To fry, 62
Chopped liver, 18
Liver in a stew, 62
Orangel iver, 62
LOBSTER: 44
To prepare, 44
Curried, 39
Devilled, 39
Lobster mornay, 44
Lobster salad, 44

LUNCHEON MEAT:
To use, 61
Barbecued, 61
Grilled with cheese, 61
Savoury puff, 61

Mackerel, 45
Marshmallow pyramids, 88
Mayonnaise cheese sauce, 74
MEAT: also see BACON, BEEF
  LAMB, etc.
Cuts of, to choose, 49
Cooking meat, 53
 To boil, 53
 Cooking in foil, 62
  Chops, 63
  Steak, 62
 To curry, 57, 58
 To fry, 53
 To grill, 53
 To reheat, 63
Cuts for frying/grilling, 54
 Accompaniments to, 54
 Prepacked, 51
Meat risotto, 78
Meat sauce: variations, 75
MELON:
As hors d'oeuvre, 13
Sherry melon, 80
With grapefruit, orange, 13
With orange, 13
With raspberry sauce, 80
With wine/sherry, 13
Mexicaine steaks, 55
Mixed hors d'oeuvre, 14
Mock Hollandaise sauce, 66
Moules marinière, 30
MUSHROOMS:
Fresh, to prepare/cook, 69
Other ways to buy, 69
Mushroom omelette, 25
Mushroom pie, 90
Mushroom soup, 19
Mustard tomato sauce, 59

Nut omelette, 84

OFFAL:
To choose, 51
Kidneys, 60
Liver, 62
Sweetbreads, 62
OMELETTES:
To make, 24
Asparagus, 25
Bacon, 25
Bread, 25
Cheese, 25
Fruit, 84
Ham, 25
Herb, 25
Ice cream, 84
Jam, 84
Jelly, 84
Mushroom, 25
Nut, 84
Orange, 84
Plain, 24
Prawn, 25
Soufflé, 24
Spanish, 25
Tomato, 25
ONION:
To minimise smell, 69
Other ways to buy, 69
Open sandwiches, 27
ORANGE:
Orange liver, 62
Orange omelette, 84
Orange salad, 71
Orange, caramelled, 79

Parmesan halibut, 42
Parsnip, 69

PASTA:
Choosing pasta: types, 73
To cook, to reheat, 72, 73
To serve as vegetable, 72
To.use canned pasta, 76
Long spaghetti, 73
Spaghetti alla marinara, 75
 With ham, 75
 With other fish, 75
Spaghetti, meat sauce, 75
 Variations, 75
Ways to serve
 With anchovy sauce. 74
 With egg sauce, 74
 With evaporated milk cheese
  sauce, 74
 With mayonnaise cheese
  sauce, 74
 With tomato sauce, 74
PÂTÉ:
Cod's roe pâté, 39
Peaches, 86
Pears in red wine, 86
PEAS:
Fresh, to prepare/cook, 69
New ways to serve, 69
Other ways to buy, 69
PEPPERS:
To prepare/cook, 69
New ways to serve, 69
Stuffed, 69, 91
Peppered steak, 54
PINEAPPLE:
To prepare fresh, 80
Pineapple fritters, 86
Pineapple, roast, 60
Plaice, 45
Plain omelette, 24
Poached cod, 38
POACHED EGGS: 23
Egg poachers, 24
On haddock, 23
Poached scallops, 47
PORK:
Cuts of, to choose, 51
Fried: variations, 55
Grilled: variations, 55
Pot roast, 59
POTATOES:
Fresh, to prepare/cook, 70
New ways to serve, 70
Other ways to buy, 70
Cheese potatoes, 70
Potato cakes, 70
Potato salad, 72
Sauté, 70
Scalloped, 70
Stuffed: variations, 70
Prawn, tomato chowder, 19
Prawn omelette, 25
PUDDINGS, hot:
Apple fritters, 86
Apple rice bake, 83
Baked apples, 85
Baked custard, 85
Banana fritters, 86
Bananas in sauce, 86
Boiled custard, 85
Bread and butter pudding, 85
Caramelled rice, 84
Chocolate custard, 85
Creamed rice, canned, 83
Crumb custard, 85
Floating islands, 85
Fruit omelette, 84
Fruit pies, 86
Ice cream omelette, 84
Jam omelette, 84
Jelly omelette, 84
Nut omelette, 84
Orange omelette, 84
Peaches, 86
Pears in red wine, 86
Pineapple fritters, 86
Ready prepared, 82
Rice souffié, 83

Rose hip, rice soufflé, 84
Spiced custard, 85
Sweet omelette, 84
Swiss roll pudding, 85
Zabaione, 86

Quick doughnuts, 87
Quick Moussaka, 60

RADISH:
To use radishes, 70
RICE:
To boil, to curry, to fry, 76, 77
Left-over, to reheat, 77
As a vegetable, 76
In a salad, 77
Caramelled, rice, 84
Kedgeree No. 1, No. 2, 77
Rice, creamed, canned, 83
Rice soufflé, 83
 Rose hip, rice soufflé, 84
Risotto, 77
 Fish, 77
 Vegetable: variations, 78
 Meat, 78
Saffron rice, 77
Roasted halibut, 42
ROES:
Cod roe, 38
 Cod's roe pâté, 39
 Creamed roe, mushroom
  sauce, 38
 Fried, 38
 Grilled, 39
  With cheese, 39
 Smoked, 39
Herring roe, 44
 Fried, 44
 Poached in milk, 44
 Steamed, 44
Russian salad, 72

Saffron rice, 77
SALADS:
Avocado, cream cheese, 72
Bean, 71
Beetroot and apple 71
Carrot, 71
Cheese, 71
Coleslaw, 71
Crab, 39
Egg, 71
Egg and anchovy, 17
Egg and cheese, 27
Fresh fruit, 91
Herring, 44
 With beetroot, 44
 With corn, 44
 With egg, 44
 With lemon or vinegar, 44
Lobster, 44
Orange, 71
Potato, 72
Russian, 72
Savoury buckling, 36
Scrambled cheese, 27
Slimming: various, 92
Tomato, 13
Salami, 14
SALMON:
Fish cakes, 46
Hash, 46
Pie, 46
 With eggs, 46
 With mushrooms, 46
 With soup, 46
Canned salmon, cold/hot, 45
 With asparagus, 45
 With mushroom, 45
 With tomato, 45
Fresh salmon cold/hot, 45
Sardine, cheese toast, 28
SAUCES:
Anchovy, 74
Barbecue, 61
Brown, 67

Cheese, 74
Curry, 58
Devilled, 39
Egg, 74
Evaporated milk cheese, 74
Mayonnaise cheese, 74
Meat, 75
Mock Hollandaise, 66
Mustard tomato, 59
Tartare, 45
Tomato cheese, 22
Tomato, 75
White—blending method, 74
White—roux method, 74
SAUSAGES:
To bake, fry, grill, 59
Toad-in-the-hole, 59
Sauté potatoes, 70
Savoury buckling salad, 36
Savoury grilled herrings, 43
Savoury poached eggs, 23
Savoury puff, 61
Scalloped potatoes, 70
SCALLOPS:
Fried, 47
Poached, 47
Scallops au gratin, 47
Scallops mornay, 47
Scampi fried in butter, 47
Scrambled cheese salad, 27
Scrambled eggs, 24
Sherry melon, 80
Slimming, rules for, 89
Smoked cod's roe, 39
Smoked haddock, mushrooms, 41
Smoked haddock, tomatoes, 41
Smoked trout, 13
Soft-boiled eggs, 21
SOLE: 47
Lemon sole mornay, 48
Sole in tomato sauce, 48
Sole with grapes, 48
SOUFFLÉS:
Asparagus, 25
Basic savoury, 25
Cheese, 26
Rice, 83
Rose hip, rice, 84
Spinach, 26
Soufflé omelette, 24
Soufflé tomato, 15
SOUPS:
Asparagus, ham chowder, 20
Asparagus, tuna chowder, 20
Bacon, potato chowder, 19
Bacon, tomato chowder, 18

Beef, mushroom, 19
Borsch, 20,
Carrot, 19
Carrot (slimming), 89
Consommé plus, 20
Corn and chicken, 20
Corn tomato, 20
Cream of mushroom, 19
Cream of vegetable, 20
Cucumber, 89
Curried, 20
Fish, 18
French onion, 89
Fruit, 89
Mushroom, 19
Prawn, tomato chowder, 19
Tomato vegetable, 20
Vegetable purée, 20
Vegetable soup, 19
With cheese, 19
Spaghetti alla marinara, 75
With ham, 75
With other fish, 75
Spaghetti, meat sauce, 75
Variations, 75
Spanish omelette, 25
Spiced custard, 85
SPINACH:
Fresh, to prepare/cook 71
Other ways to buy, 71
Spinach soufflé, 26
STEAK:
Cuts of, 50
Curried, 54
Foil cooked, 62
With red wine, 63
Without vegetables, 63
Grilled, 55
Mexicaine, 55
Peppered, 54
Steak Diane, 54
In cream/brandy, 54
In paprika sauce, 54
In sour cream, 54
In tomato purée, 54
In vegetable medley, 55
Waldorf steaks, 55
Steamed fruit cake, 87
With marmalade, 87
With mixed spice, 87
Steamed haddock, 41
With mayonnaise, 41
With mushrooms, 41
With paprika, 41
With tomato juice, 41
Steamed herring roes, 44

STEWS: (see also CASSEROLED
DISHES AND STEWS)
Stew Americaine, 57
With corned beef, 57
With kidneys, 57
With mixed vegetables, 57
Burgundy: variations, 58
STEWING STEAK, canned:
Curried, 60
Goulash, 60
Hasty Cassoulet, 60
Quick Moussaka, 60
Strawberries, 80
Stuffed aubergine, 64
Stuffed fried herrings, 43
Stuffed haddock, 41
Stuffed peppers, 69, 91
Stuffed potatoes, 70
Variations, 70
Stuffed tomatoes, 15
With ham, 15
With prawns, 15
Swede, 69
SWEETBREADS:
To blanch, 62
Fried, 62
Swiss eggs, 21
Swiss roll pudding, 85

Tartare sauce, 45
Toad-in-the-hole, 59
Toasted cheese, 28
TOMATO:
Fresh, to prepare/cook, 71
Other ways to buy tomatoes, 71
Soufflé tomatoes, 15
Stuffed, cooked, 15
Stuffed, with ham, 15
Stuffed, with prawns, 15
Stuffed, uncooked, 16
Tomato cheese sauce, 22
Tomato omelette, 25
Tomato salad, 13
With anchovy fillets, 13
With cream cheese, 13
With ham, 13
With hard-boiled egg, 13
With sardines, 13
Tomato sauce, 75
Tomato vegetable soup, 20
TONGUE, canned, cooked: 60
In cherry sauce, 61
Portuguese: variations, 61
TRIPE:
To cook, 93

TROUT:
Smoked, 49
Trout and almonds, 48
With breadcrumbs, 48
With lemon and capers, 48
Trout in cream sauce, 48
Trout in yoghurt, 48
Trout meunière, 48
TUNA: 49
Tuna eggs, 23
Turbot, 49
Turnip, 69

VEAL
Cuts of, to choose, 50
Fried, coated, 55
Variations, 55
Fried, uncoated, 55
With cream, sherry, 55
With lemon, capers, 55
With soup, 55
With tuna, cream, 55
With wine/sherry, 55
Grilled 55
With bacon, 55
With cheese, 55
With cheese and ham, 55
With mustard, 55
With yoghurt, 55
VEGETABLES: see also
ARTICHOKE,
ASPARAGUS,
AUBERGINE, etc.
Choosing, cooking, 63
Cream of vegetable soup, 20
Tomato vegetable soup, 20
Vegetable/cheese custard, 28
Vegetable hot pot, 90
Vegetable purée soup 20
Vegetable risotto, 78
Vegetable soup, 19
With cheese, 19
Vegetable toasts, 28
Vinaigrette dressing, 16

Waldorf steaks, 55
WATERCRESS:
Fresh, to prepare, 71
Welsh cakes, 87
White sauce, 74
Whiting, 49

YOGHOURT: 82
With jelly, 82
With nuts, 82
With trout, 48

Zabaione, 86